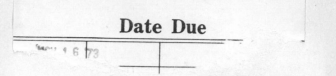

Date Due

4 6 73

The Meaning of Commercial Television

THE TEXAS-STANFORD SEMINAR, 1966

MARSHALL MC LUHAN • GEORGE SCHAEFER • DAVID POTTER

LEONARD S. MATTHEWS • THOMAS MOORE • PAUL GOODMAN

HARRY S. ASHMORE • AUGUST PRIEMER • JOHN R. SILBER

EDITED BY STANLEY T. DONNER

UNIVERSITY OF TEXAS PRESS AUSTIN & LONDON

Library of Congress Catalog Card No. 67-24134
Copyright © 1967 by the University of Texas Press
All rights reserved
Type set by G&S Typesetters, Austin
Printed by The Steck Company, Austin
Bound by Universal Bookbindery, Inc., San Antonio

PREFACE

The Texas-Stanford Seminar on "The Meaning of Commercial Television" was held at Asilomar, California, on April 24, 25, and 26, 1966. The Seminar was made possible by a grant from *TV Guide* magazine through James T. Quirk, publisher. This was the second seminar of this kind; the first was held a year earlier at the same place on the subject, "The Future of Commercial Television, 1965–1975." A third seminar, "Commercial Television in Transition," was held May 21, 22, and 23, 1967, by the two universities, again with the support of *TV Guide*. It may be that these seminars will provide the means for such a valuable exchange that they will become an annual tradition within the industry.

While the 1966 Seminar had several purposes, the main purpose was to help bring about the general improvement of television. While recognizing the great moments of significant programming, thoughtful people both within and outside the industry are of the opinion that television could be a great deal better. The central question has always been how to bring about the improvements which should be made. Efforts in this direction have not been very effective.

Even when television was new the presidents and other spokesmen of the networks and the associations talked of the high promise of television. Yet, having voiced these views from the public platform the spokesmen returned to the intense commercial pressures of their daily work and they made no noticeable change. It was not that the spokesmen did not believe in the change they were recommending, but rather that it seemed impossible to accomplish.

Professional critics, mainly from newspapers, have pointed to the shortcomings of television almost daily. However, no great improvement has resulted from these criticisms; in fact, it would seem that almost the reverse has occurred. Negative criticism of genuine efforts to provide outstanding programming has tended to discourage these efforts.

Governmental pressures for the improvement of television are usually instigated by the Federal Communications Commission and depend in good part on the vision, courage, and strength of the chairman of that commission. Over a long period of time it has become evident that these pressures have little lasting effect. An underlying fear of government encroachment causes the industry to unite in resistance to governmental pressures, even when these are brought about by justified criticism. Once the government embarks on more stringent regulation there is little hope that this regulation will be relaxed or changed later on. Concerted resistance to government pressures and regulation is understandable.

Regulatory codes have been adopted within the industry itself. These efforts at self-regulation are commendable, but they are effective only to the extent that stations subscribe to the codes and abide by them. The present regulatory codes set minimal standards and have little to do with setting goals for the improvement of television.

The purpose of the 1966 Seminar was to bring together representatives of television, the allied fields of sponsorship and advertising, and of independent producers. If there is general agreement within and without the industry that television could be better, how could improvement be made? No one person, even if he were a network president or the chairman of the FCC, could make such changes. In fact the television industry itself is so interconnected with business that it cannot make changes alone. Planned, purposeful change is possible only if the enlightened leaders of television and the businesses closely associated with television jointly arrive at agreement. If the television industry desires to improve its product, if the sponsor who is paying the bill is in agreement and is supported in his agreement by the advertising agency which represents him, and if those who prepare the programs are of the same mind, progressive improvement can be made.

The plan for the Seminar went beyond simply bringing representatives of the several groups together. These representatives had to be "the influentials," the leaders who have a voice in the policy-making decisions within their own companies. Strangely enough these seminars established the first meetings of the four groups who collectively control television. Indeed, the 1966 Seminar was the first time in seven years that the presidents of the three principal networks had met together to discuss mutual problems.

The Seminar provided a place and a climate for significant discussion. Asilomar on the California coast was ideal for reflective thought, away from the immediate pressures of daily business, away from the telephone and even from the television set. Stimuli for thought and possible action were provided in speeches by several of the nation's leading intellectuals. Group discussions followed the formal presentations. After each major presentation the fifty conferees were divided into groups of ten. Each group, under the leadership of a faculty member from The University of Texas or Stanford University, engaged in free, vigorous, and pointed discussion. The press was excluded from the Seminar, so each conferee could speak his mind without fear that ideas he expressed (possibly only to elicit counterviews) would be headlined in the paper the next day.

The content of the formal presentations, an analysis of the discussions, and a summation of the findings of the Seminar constitute the body of this report. In general the results were positive. The conferees were able, responsible leaders of their own fields, and they found the place conducive to reflection and creative thought. The formal presentations were all stimulating and some were devastatingly critical. Even so the conferees sorted out the ideas which were honest and pertinent and argued them among themselves. Part of the value of the Seminar was the opportunity it gave for men of different fields, yet of like dedication and like interests, to exchange views. Establishing a horizontal line of communication among representatives of television, advertising agencies, and independent producers was in itself a most valuable result.

Concrete action from discussion is always difficult to achieve. What final good may result from the Seminar for the television viewer will perhaps come slowly, but it will come. Conferee after conferee wrote afterward of the tremendous value of the meeting.

The Seminar was planned and presented by Stanley T. Donner, director, from The University of Texas, and Henry Breitrose, assistant director, from Stanford University. Arthur Shulman, assistant to the publisher of *TV Guide* served as liaison between the two universities and *TV Guide*. The Advisory Board for the seminar were Bob Banner, Bob Banner Associates; Stanley T. Donner, The University of Texas; George Laboda, Colgate Palmolive Company; Donald McGannon, Westinghouse Broadcasting Company; Leonard Matthews, Leo Burnett Company; James T. Quirk, *TV Guide*; and Richard Salant, Columbia Broadcasting System.

The participants in the Seminar were:

GERARD APPY
Director of Field Service
National Educational Television

EDWARD BLEIER
Vice President
American Broadcasting Company

RICHARD C. BLOCK
Vice President and General Manager
Kaiser Broadcasting

NORMAN E. CASH
President
Television Bureau of Advertising, Inc.

SAMUEL E. CHARLTON
Vice President, Marketing
Humble Oil and Refining Company

DONALD L. CLARK
Vice President
Xerox Corporation

DAVID DORTORT
Producer of *Bonanza*

DON DURGIN
President
National Broadcasting Company

NORMAN FELTON
President
Arena Productions, Inc.

JAMES S. FISH
Vice President, Advertising and
    Marketing Services
General Mills, Inc.

FRANK P. FOGARTY
President
Meredith Broadcasting Company

E. P. GENOCK
Director of Television Advertising
Eastman Kodak Company

DAVID GERBER
Vice President
Twentieth Century-Fox Television, Inc.

FREDERICK S. GILBERT
Vice President and General Manager
Time-Life Broadcasting, Inc.

PAUL HENNING
Paul Henning Productions

PHILIP B. HINERFELD
Vice President, Advertising
Pepsi-Cola Company

ROY HUGGINS
Roncon Films-Huggins Production

MARVIN KOSLOW
Corporate Director of Advertising
Bristol-Myers Company

LEONARD S. MATTHEWS
Executive Vice President
Leo Burnett Company, Inc.

WILLARD A. MICHAELS
Vice President—Television Division
Storer Broadcasting Company

THOMAS W. MOORE
President
American Broadcasting Company

JOHN J. MORRISSEY
Director, Advertising & Sales
    Promotion Office
Ford Motor Company

LYLE NELSON
Director of University Relations
Stanford University

MERRILL PANITT
Editor
TV Guide Magazine

EDWARD J. PECHIN
Assistant Director of Advertising
E. I. Du Pont de Nemours & Company

C. WREDE PETERSMEYER
President
Corinthian Broadcasting Company

RICHARD A. R. PINKHAM
Senior Vice President in Charge of
    Media and Programs
Ted Bates and Company, Inc.

AUGUST PRIEMER
Director of Marketing Services
S. C. Johnson and Son, Inc.

I. A. QUACKENBOSS
Vice President, Marketing Services
Johnson and Johnson

JAMES T. QUIRK
Publisher
TV Guide Magazine

LEE M. RICH
President
Mirisch-Rich Television Productions

LAWRENCE H. ROGERS, II
President
Taft Broadcasting Company

HAROLD E. SAVAGE
Advertising Section
General Motors Corporation

GEORGE SCHAEFER
President
Compass Productions, Inc.
Producers of *Hallmark Hall of Fame*

EDGAR J. SCHERICK

JOHN A. SCHNEIDER
President, CBS Broadcast Group
Columbia Broadcasting System, Inc.

AL SIMON
President
Filmways TV Productions, Inc.

J. E. SLATER
Associate Director
The Ford Foundation

SAMUEL THURM
Vice President, Advertising
Lever Brothers Company, Inc.

JACK TIPTON
General Manager
KLZ-TV, Denver, Colorado

H. TRAVIESAS
Vice President
Batten, Barton, Durstine & Osborn, Inc.

MARTIN UMANSKY
Vice President and General Manager
KAKE-TV and Radio, Wichita, Kansas

HATHAWAY WATSON
President
RKO General Broadcasting

DAVID WINDLESHAM
Programme Director
Rediffusion Television, England

ROBERT D. WOOD
Vice President and General Manager
KNXT—CBS Television Stations,
    Los Angeles, California

The faculty members who guided the discussions in the various groups of the Seminar were Henry Breitrose, Stanford University; Martin Maloney, Northwestern University; Nathan Maccoby, Stanford University; and John Meaney and Robert Schenkkan, The University of Texas. Five graduate students from Stanford and five from The University of Texas assisted the directors, the faculty, and the conferees during the Seminar. The student aides from Stanford University were Stephen Longstreth, Evaristo Obregon, Charles Selden, Bonnie Sherr, and Christopher Tillam. Those from The University

of Texas were David Grimland, Phillip Miller, Sharon Rountree, Lee
Salzberger, and Joseph Walters.

The program of the Seminar began on Sunday evening with wel-
coming addresses by Kenneth Cuthbertson, vice president of Stanford
University, and Norman Hackerman, vice chancellor of The University of Texas. The keynote address was delivered by Harry S. Ashmore, Pulitzer Prize winner and now of the Center for the Study of
Democratic Institutions. On Monday morning representatives of television and the three allied businesses gave presentations, each describing the function of television from his particular point of interest.
George Schaefer of Compass Productions spoke for the independent
television producers; the sponsors were represented by August
Priemer of S. C. Johnson and Son, Inc.; the advertising agencies,
by Leonard S. Matthews of Leo Burnett Company; and the television
industry by Thomas Moore of the American Broadcasting Company.

The afternoon was given over to an examination of the meaning
of television from the broad view. David Potter, an historian from
Stanford University, placed television in perspective. He was followed
by Paul Goodman of the Institute for Policy Studies and at that time a
visiting professor at San Francisco State College. His was a personal
view drawn from and supported by both sociology and politics.

In the evening Marshall McLuhan spoke on the subject of "Television in a New Light." His thought-provoking ideas carried beyond
his particular way of looking at television to his new researches in
sensory profiles.

The Seminar moved from the keynote to the examination of the
meaning of television by its practitioners to a discussion of the broad
view of television. In the final formal speech, on Tuesday, John R.
Silber of The University of Texas established a philosophical base for
his appraisal of individual television programs and television as a
whole. The discussion concluded by examining the meaning of tele-

vision from a personal view. Stanley T. Donner of The University of Texas, Director of the Seminar, gave a short summary speech at the final dinner.

The primary purpose of the formal presentations was to develop ideas, to raise questions, or to evoke emotional response. In some cases the speeches accomplished all three goals. The main work of the Seminar took place in the group meetings which followed the general discussion of each formal presentation. In addition to a faculty member who served as discussion leader, each group had a *rapporteur*. It was his responsibility to record any consensus that his group might have reached and to report the findings of all discussions before a plenary session held during the last afternoon.

This publication of the results of the Seminar has been aided by the efforts of many people. In particular, the analyses of the group discussions were made possible by the careful records kept by the *rapporteurs*: Norman Cash of the Television Bureau of Advertising; Donald Clark of Xerox Corporation; Norman Felton of Arena Productions, Inc.; Leonard Matthews of Leo Burnett Company; and David Windlesham of Rediffusion Television, London. *TV Guide* magazine generously helped to defray the publication costs. Special recognition is also due to Mrs. Barry Cole for her valuable editorial assistance in the preparation of the manuscript.

S. T. D.

CONTENTS

THE MOURNFUL NUMBERS

HARRY S. ASHMORE

The Mournful Numbers

Just a year ago [1965] David Brinkley and I were called upon to open the annual convention of my old fraternity, the American Society of Newspaper Editors. Our assignment, as the program had it, was to stretch the assembled brethren on the analyst's couch.

In the spirit, and the jargon, of the occasion, I charged the editors with "creating an illusion of controversy as a painless substitute for the real thing. This makes you feel even better during the rest of the convention when the politicians who follow this panel tell you how great, and good, and free, and indispensable you are."

The muted *mea culpa*—the public confession of a little guilt—is, of course, not unusual these days and is generally considered sound public relations as well as good group therapy. But it may have been noteworthy that the editors of the nation's metropolitan newspapers also felt it necessary to make a gesture of assurance to the public— and, I suspect, to themselves—that they were being subjected to genuine 100-proof criticism, not the self-serving brand usually offered on such occasions. Thus they included in their analysts' panel a conspicuous and sometimes acerbic commentator from the competitive medium, and a renegade editor no longer beholden to any newspaper publisher.

I assume my assignment this evening is of the same order. Surely such a distinguished assemblage from broadcasting and allied industries does not need to be told what's *right* with commercial television. By all quantitative standards television is enjoying an enormous success, having acquired the biggest audience, sales impact, gross income, and net earnings in the history of mass communications. And, in case of any lingering insecurity occasioned by the relative youth of the medium, the Television Information Office has a survey showing that television has finally pulled past newspapers in something the Roper Poll calls "believability."

Read in another context, however, the numbers that gladden the hearts of cost accountants and stockholders are as mournful as those cited by Longfellow to describe an empty dream. Only a few weeks ago Chairman Henry of the Federal Communications Commission diagnosed the primary affliction of the National Association of Broadcasters as "numbers neurosis"—and credited the term to the chairman of the American Association of Advertising Agencies. Mr. Henry, like all outspoken FCC chairmen, promptly abandoned the office, but the charge is harder to down than its perpetrator. Numbers can only measure commercial success, and it appears that commercialism is precisely what causes the industry's neurosis.

The symptoms that interest me, and should concern you, are those that show up within the broadcasting family. There is, for example, the testimony of Stan Freberg, who makes a very handsome living fabricating television commercials. Mr. Freberg offered his view in *TV Guide*, which hardly can be said to be hostile to the source of its mother's milk. "Madison Avenue and the networks have conspired to make commercial television a dreadful, deadly place indeed," Mr. Freberg wrote. "I should like to officially declare commercial television a disaster area."

Mr. Freberg is an egghead of sorts and, despite his income, perhaps open to suspicion of intellectual dissidence. But there are also expressions of concern from persons of impeccable self-interest. For example, here is a comment from Sherman J. McQueen, vice-president and director of broadcasting for Foote, Cone and Belding, directed at the very jugular vein of the industry. "Frankly, agency people are embarrassed by the majority of the commercials on television today," he said, in an interview with the *Los Angeles Times*. "I wish there were a trend away from all this clutter. We seem to be headed toward more commercialism, and that disturbs me."

David Karp, in the *New York Times Magazine*, has provided a clinical study of the effect of the "numbers neurosis" on commercial television's creative talent. Mr. Karp notes that when he joined the industry as a writer in 1950 television's total annual income was 170.8 million dollars. In the course of fifteen years of unbroken progress to last year's 2.5 *billion* dollar income, Mr. Karp and his creative colleagues have had to acquire an understanding of the real meaning of these large numbers. This was necessary to their survival since they found themselves dealing with those whom Mr. Karp describes as "intelligent, well-educated, carefully combed and curried men who love such numbers and who write them down and add them up and who chuckle over them softly. They are numbers which have meaning and importance to these men."

That meaning, Mr. Karp discovered, is that while art forms and aesthetics and even entertainment are all right in their place, their place is not in commercial television, which is an advertising medium. The inescapable lesson of experience, he asserts, is that quality in commercial television programming not only has nothing to do with success, but actually may be a distraction. Here is how he chronicles the end result of the "numbers neurosis" for his own profession:

A labor relations negotiator for one of the major television networks pointed out that a survey of TV audiences revealed that it did not matter which writer wrote any particular episode of a TV dramatic series. The quality of one writer's contribution over another had no demonstrable effect upon the show's rating. It was said without malice, and accepted without regret by the writer-members of the negotiating team which faced him across the table.

Balzac might have wept; Dickens might have grown white with rage; and Hemingway might have punched him in the face. TV writers are a tougher breed. They pressed their lips together and pushed on to more pragmatic matters, determined to squeeze from their cut-rate Medicis the best price they could get for their creative agony and ecstasy.

Mr. Karp has the impressive intellectual credentials of one who is, or was, a novelist of the first rank. It is, therefore, particularly significant that he is even rougher on his aesthetic compatriots than he is on network vice presidents. Snobbish disdain for popular taste, he contends, has led the high-toned critics to denigrate the good in television along with the bad. He writes:

Their sneering helped to dry up its early chances. Now the medium has grown immensely and vulgarly and all of the numbers have doubled, quadrupled, and the business is largely an expression of cost accounting, and the intellectual establishment is infuriated that it has not disappeared . . . The emotional anger that lies at the heart of most intellectuals when they think about television is not its lack of quality, but its booming, bouncing, vigorous success.

I think Mr. Karp is entirely correct. One of the several tragedies visible in the wake of television's explosive take-over of mass communications is the continuing failure of the intellectual community to deal with the rude newcomer in terms that take into account the realities of the mass audience the medium is designed to serve. Much published criticism is ostensibly based on standards so esoteric as to be irrelevant, or, worse still, reflects the insufferable condescension of an exalted spirit nobly doing intellectual social work among the less fortunate. Such closet criticism cannot conceivably arouse any response from television's vast audience. Thus this spate of elegant sarcasm and earnest exhortation produces nothing more than an occasional fit of petulance among a few sentimental television proprietors and executives.

There still are, however, a few able and sturdy critics, mostly on newspapers, who measure programming against standards commensurate with the norms of popular American taste. If they insist, quite properly, that television ought to exert some effort to raise these norms they do not demand a great aesthetic leap forward that would leave most of the existing audience behind. These realists may be, and often are, heard sympathetically in television's executive suites. Yet as we read the mournful numbers we have to conclude that the pragmatists are no more effective than the effete scolds of the literary circuit. Put a legitimate complaint of sloppy writing, imitative plotting, indifferent acting, sleazy production, and general vulgarity against a high Nielsen rating and there is no contest. The answer comes back in the title of David Karp's *New York Times* piece: "TV Shows Are Not Supposed To Be Good—They Are Supposed To Make Money."

It seems to me that any serious consideration of the meaning of commercial television has to begin with recognition that Mr. Karp's proposition is substantially correct. The window dressing with which television's hired apologists attempt to disguise the real meaning of the mournful numbers has become thin and transparent. The response to every exposure of mis- or malfeasance is to break out the flag of self-regulation, resoundingly equated with liberty, justice, democracy, and free enterprise. But at the NAB convention, Chairman Henry kicked the stuffing out of what he called the "Alphonse and Gaston Act" devised not long ago to immunize the industry's 190-million-dollar income from tobacco advertising against the possible effects of lung cancer. Mr. Henry said: "The truth is that the broadcast industry has not only failed to pass this test of self-regulation; it has not even taken it. The industry's self-regulation not only lacks teeth; it has bleeding gums. Moreover, it fools no one."

Self-regulation has not worked even when the issue pits the self-interest of the advertiser, who pays the freight, against that of the broadcaster, who insists on determining the payload. It was largely at the behest of advertisers, who object to having their own expensive sales messages lost in a clutter of commercials, that the NAB adopted a governing code. This agreement requires members in good standing to limit commercials to a total of five minutes ten seconds, including station-break time, in each prime half-hour. Only broadcasters who observe the code are entitled to display the NAB's Seal of Good Practice—and in Los Angeles alone the seal has been abandoned by four of seven local stations. These have now pushed the commercial clutter up to an average of six-and-a-half minutes per prime half-hour. Presumably for public-relations reasons, the three network stations are still holding the line, and bearing the seal. But on another front ABC broke through the accepted limitation by interrupting *Batman* for a fourth commercial, and Walter Cronkite at CBS has had to yield on the previous four-commercial limit to admit the fifth that already had found acceptance on NBC's *Huntley-Brinkley*.

No one, as Chairman Henry has said, is being fooled, and I hope that at least we are coming to the end of this sort of blatant insult to the public intelligence. I would like to think the outer limit of absurdity was reached at the same NAB convention when the president of the order, Vincent Wasilewski, called upon Congress to enact new laws to halt FCC interference with programming. "Nail down with absolute finality," Mr. Wasilewski demanded, "that the constitutional protections of free press which cover print media are every bit as applicable to broadcasting." I trust I will be forgiven the asperity of a battle-scarred veteran of the civil liberties front when I observe that this is the first attempt I can recall to use a dead horse for stalking purposes. No one of consequence has ever suggested that the constitutional protection accorded the print media does not apply to broadcasting. There is only one such protection—a guarantee against governmental censorship—and in the unlikely event that the FCC ever attempted to use its regulatory power to censor a television program for political reasons no one can doubt the reaction of our libertarian Supreme Court. I will, indeed, personally guarantee to produce a platoon of writ-bearing lawyers from the American Civil Liberties Union at the first faint sign of such intervention.

The truth, as told by the mournful numbers, and confirmed by the brief careers of the outspoken chairmen, Minow and Henry, is that for all practical purposes the FCC is the creature of the broadcasting industry. And if the agency should ever get out of hand there are enough owned and operated Congressmen to bring it promptly back to heel.

The industry, in short, has achieved an effective state of immunity, not only from adverse regulation, but from the criticism of competitive media and of disgruntled creative spirits within its own ranks. This impervious condition is finally buttressed by a virtual exemption from any adverse effects of the economic law of supply and demand. What government regulation does provide is the limitation on the availability of broadcast channels that produces a golden scramble for their advertising services.

It is the very dimensions of television's monumental success that should lend a new urgency to the confused public discussion of the ultimate impact of the new medium upon society at large. Until lately the complacent could and did ignore broadcasting's offenses on the ground that television was only one of many voices competing for public attention. However, in commenting on the survey that demonstrates television's lead position in mass communications, Burns Roper suggested that the medium could no longer be regarded as,

> just a passer of idle time or a tool to sell things; I believe it will increasingly play a key role in the transmission of ideas . . . We have reached a point, not where television is about to become a teacher instead of a plaything, but where television is increasingly being turned to as the *complete* medium, capable of satisfying the needs for both fantasy *and* information.

I believe Mr. Roper is correct. I believe, indeed, that we are already there—that the picture of the great world held by most Americans is primarily shaped and colored by the sights and sounds that reach them through the electronic media. There is a conscious, but I fear waning effort to fill in this picture by presenting live coverage of important events, by attempting serious commentary on the news, by preparing occasional inspired and provocative documentaries, and by assembling thoughtful men to discuss serious matters before the cameras. Such programming, however, is consigned to a sort of sideshow by the "numbers game," which proves that these programs attract audiences so small they cannot pay their own way. The bland situation comedies, the turgid soap operas, the westerns and the private eyes and the monsters and the hillbillies, the teenagers writhing through the frugathons, and yattering daytime people trailing among the studio audience, and the slick comedians with the light blue jokes —all these also are painting a compelling picture of the world for the average American family that now spends an average of five-and-a-half hours before the set on an average day. If Mr. Roper is right this soon will be the *only* picture exposed to many, maybe to most, Americans by the complete medium which brings them both fantasy and information—and with magnificent impartiality leaves it up to the viewer to figure out which is which.

Father Thomas Merton has described the result in prophetic terms:

Clearly, the "powers of the air" and "elements" which in Paul's day dominated men's minds through pagan religion or through religious legalism, today dominate us in the confusion and ambiguity of the Babel of tongues we call mass-society. Certainly I do not condemn everything in the mass media. But how does one stop to separate the truth from the half-truth, the event from the pseudo-event, reality from the manufactured image? It is in this confusion of images and myths, superstitions and ideologies that the "powers of the air" govern our thinking—even our thinking about religion! Where there is no critical perspective, no detached observation, no time to ask the pertinent questions, how can one avoid being deluded and confused?

The dark possibilities of the "powers of the air" now being unleashed by the new technology are recognized by many influential people in broadcasting, and I have no doubt that their concern is genuine. But a dominant characteristic of broadcasting is the manner in which mushroom growth has diffused responsibility. It is almost literally true that nothing of consequence that happens on a network is any single person's fault. When I talked with Fred Friendly a few weeks after his spectacular resignation from CBS he conceded that even the extreme gesture makes no difference. "This is the hardest thing of all to accept—that at every level, right up to the top, we are all interchangeable parts."

To speak seriously of self-regulation as a safeguard against the dark "powers of the air" presupposes that the industry has the internal capacity to undertake dispassionate analysis of the social effects of the vast influence it wields—that is, to determine the public good and respect it even when it means some diminution of profits. This clearly is impossible so long as the numbers neurosis is rampant, for the numbers allow only two value judgments and determine these with an adding machine—an up-trend is good, a down-trend is bad. In any event, with the best will in the world, I doubt that critical analysis is possible for Fred Friendly's interchangeable parts. Father Merton's final question applies with special force to those who operate in the high tension of television's upper brackets: "Where there is no critical perspective, no detached observation, no time to ask the pertinent questions, how can one avoid being deluded and confused?"

I cannot bring you a new solution to this besetting problem. I can only urge you to seriously and dispassionately examine an old one— the proposal brought forth twenty years ago by the Commission on Freedom of the Press. The Commission firmly disposed of the ideological argument that is usually employed as a calculated diversion in the running debate on this issue. Government, the Commission held, cannot and should not act in the critical area that borders on censorship. At the same time, the Commission contended, it is evident that the public cannot continue to rely on the media to set their own standards and police their own performance. The Commission's answer was the establishment of an agency wholly independent of both government and industry, without powers of enforcement but armed with great prestige, to report regularly on the performance of mass communications as a whole. The goal is a communications system that matches its freedom with responsibility.

The Commission's report, published under the title *A Free and Responsible Press*, immediately aroused a storm of protest from the media, and as a result, financial support was never available to carry through its recommendations. Yet, almost everyone who thinks seriously about the state of our communications system in terms of the public interest sooner or later comes back to some version of the basic idea. Jack Gould, commenting in the *New York Times* on the new study of educational television undertaken by the Carnegie Corporation, concluded that "it is regrettable that the Carnegie Corporation did not go all-out and set up a National Commission on Television. Such a body could make periodic assessments of all forms

of the medium, a variation of a British royal commission . . ." And
Hal Humphrey, putting a pox on both the broadcasters and the FCC,
wrote in the *Los Angeles Times*:

> The late President Kennedy was talking about an arts and cul-
> tural committee of private citizens who could talk directly to peo-
> ple like TV presidents on their own level. This idea seems to
> have died with Kennedy, but something like it soon must be re-
> vived and fulminated before the public voice in the communica-
> tions and arts fields is stifled forever. It takes an organized lobby
> in Washington to get your case heard . . .

The founding session of this seminar, held here at Asilomar last
year, heard a variation of the proposal from a member of the original
Commission, Professor Harold Lasswell of Yale. The reaction of the
group, as recorded in the proceedings, seems to have been based on
the usual misapprehensions—rejecting the proposal on the ground
that "there are enough regulatory bodies now and another one would
not cure any ills whatever they might be." The *rapporteur*, however,
went on to record what I regard as mild support for what Professor
Lasswell actually was talking about: "Even so there might be some
use in placing systematic criticism of television in the hands of
knowledgeable and practical, public-spirited people."

A man who would, I think, meet this group's test of knowledge-
ability, practicality, and public spirit has been largely responsible for
keeping the commission proposal alive across these twenty years.
William Benton's unshakable faith in the utility of such a commission
is based on his experience as a leading advertising executive and
publisher, reinforced by his service as Assistant Secretary of State for
Information, United States Senator, and ambassador to UNESCO. On
behalf of the Benton Foundation I have spent a good deal of time exploring the possibility of establishing the proposed critical agency in
association with a university. In a circuit of the Ivy League, and ex-

cursions elsewhere, I have found a good deal of sympathy, but no tangible support. There are, of course, good conventional reasons why a university should be reluctant to join in such an unconventional enterprise. But perhaps more compelling is the understandable prudence of administrators who know that the undertaking is inherently controversial, and certain to involve powerful men who have the means to talk back in loud and penetrating voices. One weary university president told me sadly, "Of course it ought to be done, and I'll be glad to sit as an individual on such a commission. But I've just got too damned much trouble on my hands already to think of giving you houseroom on this campus."

I have never understood why the idea of collective judgment regularly rendered has aroused so much apprehension among those who agree that stringent criticism of the media is very much in order. The proposed commission would have no power to censor, only to expose, complain, praise, and exhort—to perform, that is, on behalf of the mass media the functions the media presume to perform on behalf of all other institutions colored in any way with the public interest. The formal trappings of the commission are intended to give it sufficient prestige to meet powerful adversaries on fairly equal terms, and guarantee that its findings cannot simply be ignored. The importance of this is demonstrated by the unseemly performance of the NAB, which I have cited above. The organized broadcasters, like the editors and publishers before them, provide the most convincing demonstration that effective criticism can only come from sources outside the media's immediate orbit, and wholly independent of it. I was a member of the American Society of Newspaper Editors when *A Free and Responsible Press* [1946] was published, and I saw the august membership huddle, rumps together, horns out, in the immemorial manner of, say, the National Association of Manufacturers faced by a threat of regulated prices. When, in the ASNE *Bulletin,* I suggested that there might be some merit in the Commission report I was roundly denounced for fouling my own nest. We had reached a point where you could not tell the editors' society from the publishers' association without a program.

This blind, angry reaction served to reduce the Commission's proposal to a sort of shibboleth; the test of loyalty was to denounce it out of hand, and in a curious way it became the special target of sensitive and frustrated men who privately recognize the media's grave deficiencies but feel constrained to publicly deny their existence. In any detached appraisal I believe the passage of these twenty years provides ample evidence to refute the specious arguments of the early days. Even those who still contend that the media are doing the best they can rarely argue that the best is good enough. With the entry of the great, bland behemoth of television the stultifying tendencies cited by the Commission in 1946 have been accentuated; with three giant broadcasting corporations dominating the bulk of the programming available to Americans, the existence of centralized control, conformity, and vulgarization of public taste has become inescapably self-evident. We are confronted by a communications system that already comes very close to providing a circus to accompany the bread promised to all by the Great Society.

The pursuit of excellence has become a fashionable undertaking, or at least a fashionable phrase. But in our modern society no man can pursue excellence undeterred and uninfluenced by the image-building, taste-setting, attention-diverting system of communications that reaches out to him wherever he may be. In making the case for the establishment of a commission to the universities I have argued that academic self-interest does not deny but rather commands concern and support: teachers have access to their students' minds for only a few hours out of a lifetime, but the media reach them always and forever; and the values and standards of *academe* cannot long stand inviolate if they are hopelessly at odds with those that prevail in the market place.

No one has ever argued that there is a perfect solution to the issue that is not only critical in its own right but symbolizes, and in a sense summarizes those that now divide the world. The flyleaf of *A Free and Responsible Press* bears this quotation from John Adams, dated 1815:

> If there is ever to be an amelioration of the condition of mankind, philosophers, theologians, legislators, politicians and moralists will find that the regulation of the press is the most difficult, dangerous and important problem they have to resolve. Mankind cannot now be governed without it, nor at present with it.

The problem has not been resolved, and I do not believe the most sanguine philosophers, theologians, legislators, politicans, and moralists can argue that it has become less urgent. It is in this light that the proposal for a commission on the mass media deserves the serious consideration it has never had. At the very least the proposal for a commission stands as an inescapable challenge to all those who profess concern with the low state of the media along with their devotion to the American tradition of the free and independent press. I have heard much argument that this is a good idea whose time has not yet come, but I have seen no evidence and heard of no alternative.

DISCUSSION

There was no question about the effect of Harry Ashmore's address on the audience. Even during the speech it was clear that the audience was hostile to his proposal for the establishment of a commission for communication. Everyone was stirred, and most were stirred to anger. Ashmore had identified himself as a newspaper editor and in that sense was in the same communications camp as his listeners. In speaking of the reaction of newspaper publishers and editors to the suggestion of the Commission on the Freedom of the Press made twenty years ago he anticipated the reaction of this audience. In fact, Harold Lasswell had made a similar proposal to the Seminar a year before and it was as coolly received. While the position Ashmore took was fair enough, those who heard him were not mollified, for Ashmore's language was strong and some of it "loaded."

While most opposition expressed in the general discussion was on the emotional level, some important points were raised. It would be most difficult for a commission of ten or twenty people to set standards for an entire population. Programs with standards of high intellectual quality, such as those urged by the elite, have consistently failed to attract the mass audience. Since television is only one medium it cannot assume the responsibility for public taste, but as it moves toward becoming the complete medium its responsibilities increase. It is most difficult for television to appeal to several different tastes at once as is done in the print media. The establishment of a fourth network dedicated to minority tastes was suggested. Perhaps the most telling argument was that, historically, such distinguished and knowledgeable commissions as Ashmore would call on have usually been proved wrong in artistic matters.

The basic reason for the resistance to Ashmore's ideas is not hard to identify. While any broadcaster—at least after reflection—would consider himself a communicator, he would, in the first instance, consider himself a businessman. Few businessmen would welcome any suggestion proposing a high-level body to advise, recommend, and criticize the conduct of his business. The sensitivity of the broadcaster is heightened because his business is already subject to review by the government and by his own self-regulatory agencies. It would be possible for the telecaster to consider the suggestion for a commission after he had removed his businessman's hat and put on his communicator's hat and with it the assumption of his responsibilities to the general public.

And this is what happened, at least in part. During the discussions of the next two days questions were raised as to the ways in which a commission might be helpful. Could a commission help by designating in advance programs of special merit? Would the endorsement of a commission help to support and promote a program? Should the industry set up a study committee of its own to make recommendations before Congress does? Even those who made tentative remarks favoring a commission bogged down at the point of describing how it might be established.

At the very least Mr. Ashmore's address stirred the Seminar group and, beneath the emotional surface, raised the issue that the businessman-communicator must consider: his fundamental obligation to the public and what means can be found to help him meet this responsibility.

TELEVISION FROM THE INSIDE

GEORGE SCHAEFER

The Independent Producer

I represent the independent producer. We are known as "independents" because every move we make is dependent on a network, a sponsor, an agency, or a rating system. A more accurate description would probably be, "Producers not directly on the payroll of sponsor, network, or agency." This covers considerable territory—from the massive dispensers of quantity such as Revue, Desilu, Four Star, MGM-TV, and Twentieth Century-Fox Television, to the more restricted operations such as Disney, Wolper, Banner, Jaffe, and Compass. It does not exclude very private companies such as the one Martin Erlichmann and Barbra Streisand have formed to produce one show a year. These are all corporations offering services or completed shows, usually in association with one of the networks, but with at least some independence.

The influence of the gigantic independent is at a peak today. The influence of the small independent, which was considerable in television's first decade, has declined rapidly, starting from the day when the major studios discovered that this thing called "residual" could dwarf the income from feature pictures. The list of active independents at one time included, among many others, Bob Banner Associates, Robert Saudek Associates, Talent Associates, Herbert Brodkin's Plautus Productions, Milberg Productions, Franklin Schaffner and Fielder Cook's Directors' Company, and my own company, Compass Productions.

Today the small independent must cope with network controlled programming as well as the power of the gigantic independent, and his chances of survival are pretty slim. Most of the companies just listed have gone out of business or have been absorbed in stock transfers with major studios. This is not a healthy situation but I see little chance of immediate improvement, in spite of distressed grumblings by the FCC and the tiresome protests of those who write regularly to *TV Guide* deploring the lost "golden era."

The operation at Compass is modest and hardly typical, but I think it is safe to say that all independents work within some variation of these elements. Seven years ago Compass Productions opened offices at Columbus Circle in New York. We have a permanent staff of nine, which includes business management, an associate producer, an associate director, story and casting departments, secretaries, a receptionist, and myself. We expand when necessary and use part-time legal and accounting services. We have been active and reasonably successful in various forms of show business including Broadway and films, and even managed to survive a traumatic encounter with the New York World's Fair. The primary concentration of Compass, however, has been producing the *Hallmark Hall of Fame* for television.

This unique series, now in its fifteenth year, averages five 90-minute shows a year. They are usually plays, either adaptations or originals, and are pretaped in color using electronic cameras. In earlier days the shows were live, and one show was filmed. The sponsor is the Hallmark Greeting Card Company of Kansas City, the agency is the Chicago office of Foote, Cone and Belding, and the network is NBC. Compass supplies all above-the-line elements and NBC the below-the-line, with the average actual show costing around 250 thousand dollars, to which is added air time, promotion, and agency commission. Above-the-line elements include cast, script, producer, director, staff, rights, and musical score; below-the-line are all facilities, tape costs, scenery, costumes, and NBC personnel.

Compass budgets and is responsible, both artistically and financially, for the entire show. A firm price is quoted which varies with each program, and profit depends on staying within the budget. In recent years Compass has been producing only three new Hallmark shows a season, each taking six or seven weeks to complete. Only three weeks are spent in actual rehearsal and taping. An equal amount of time is required for preparation; editing and scoring usually take four to five days. Compass would like to expand its television activity with other special shows or perhaps a weekly series, but so far attempts to sell a series which we considered challenging have not met with success.

One of the great advantages of being small and comparatively independent is that we can afford to take considerably greater artistic risks than can any network or corporate structure which is controlled by a board of directors and answerable to stockholders. It is not hard to understand why most sponsors and networks are reasonably secure in the game of rating roulette only if they have a chip on both red and black. In fact, they often sneak a small one on zero as "insurance." You never actually win this way, but the losses are slight. The independent can occasionally put both chips on a single number and if it hits, the air waves tingle. Our latest effort was one only an independent producer backed by a brave individual sponsor would have attempted. It was a most expensive 90-minute costume drama, wherein the first groping of science into outer space is crushed by the Catholic Church with the argument that once people start to think that way, it won't be long before they'll be saying "God is dead." The fascinating aspect of this story is that the Church saw the future with such clarity, and Pope Urban's tragedy is as great as is that of Galileo. The play would not have been produced, no matter how eager this independent had been, without solid agency support and Mr. Joyce Hall's courage. While I suspect the production has alienated a few hundred viewers, I am confident it has been a memorable experience for millions.

Entertainment is said to be one of the world's two oldest professions. From Greek and Roman times to the First World War it was a reasonably straightforward attempt by a few independent creators and interpreters to amuse, move, or instruct their contemporaries, and perhaps make the world a little wiser or happier. The advent of silent movies, radio, talkies, and finally television has turned show business into big business, and the direct personal channel of entertainment has been clouded by a number of considerations that have separated creator and audience. Success in American commercial television in 1966 is measured not by the content and artistry of the program or by how much it has meant to an individual viewer, but either by its ability to attract a maximum number of sets-in-use, or by its ability to move a product off a store shelf, or even by the ingenuity with which it utilizes a studio's permanent sets and contract players.

However, let me make it clear that Compass Productions also is in business primarily to make profit. Of course we are happy when we get a high rating, as we are pleased when the sponsor and agency applaud. But our greatest satisfaction is in receiving letters from individuals for whom our work has had significance and who have bothered to write. It is only then the independent producer becomes a link in that long historic chain called "entertainment," and feels reasonably sure to which of those oldest professions commercial television belongs.

During a long trip from New York to California by way of London, Cairo, and Tokyo we noted that a high tower from which to send the signal, and the clutter of home aerials wherever you look, have become the universal symbols of civilization. One afternoon, driving north of Beirut, I stopped the car to stare in amazement at a group of tin and cardboard lean-tos in which you would hesitate to house a dog, each with a towering television antenna. Even the classic Japanese skyline is gridded for color reception and it would have been no surprise to learn that the Sphinx had been been fitted with a portable 10-inch set. The channels for mass universal communication at a personal home-to-home level will be complete in a very few years, and we may then learn just how many of the world's problems do stem from lack of direct contact between peoples. The potential power of this circuit is an H-bomb that can be used either to destroy civilization or propel it to previously undreamed-of levels. Those of us in commercial television should begin to spend time and effort planning ways to bring about the latter. Surely we can be more effective at this than any government agency, whose motives will be suspect. To counteract the impotence we all feel in the face of possible atomic destruction, let's tackle something just as powerful that can be ours to shape.

AUGUST PRIEMER

The Advertiser

The media directors of the advertising business, whom I represent, are extremely influential in the television economy. We deal with the purely commercial aspects of advertising. There is no glamour in a media director's job; we make a major contribution, we think, but we make it in a very oblique way. First of all, we determine to a major degree what the media expenditure level will be. We select the appropriate medium for the advertiser. We determine what the patterns of usage will be, whether we will turn off the money in the summer, or the winter, or whenever it is right for our product. In these three ways we obviously exert some influence on television.

In trying to develop insights into real media values, we stimulate the sellers of the media to produce information, real or imaginary, about what they have to offer. Presumably this information feeds back into an understanding body of people involved in the media who have their own products to sell. We feed back this same information to the creators of product advertising copy. In these respects we influence the commercial creativity, which is such a major part of television. We play the role of lobbyist. We also feed back the advertising economics of the media. The media must know whether they are priced to continue to serve as vehicles for commercials. It would be extremely dangerous for a medium to price itself out of commercialism without knowing it. We manipulate buying pressure, presumably by knowing alternate media paths at times when prices go beyond the realistic horizon, and in this way we affect price loads.

Finally, we have what I call the watchdog role. When we are impressed with the conversation that goes on about television—that it is cluttered, that it is losing its vitality, that it is only for children and for those who have minds of children—we feel that we must be alert to see if this is the truth. Johnson's Wax has three advertising agencies. This year, each of them was assigned a specific role in a program to alert us on the possible diminishing vitality of television. I think that what we have found so far, from everything that is available whether it be right or wrong, is that television is no less vital this year than it was last year. This was hard for us to believe. There was a lot of noise; there was a lot of thunder and lightning, but no rain.

What does television mean to us? The first two points are very obvious and always mentioned. Television is an attractive medium because it is a mass medium in quantity and frequency. It talks to a lot of people. It talks to them often. The medium is extremely suited to low-interest products because it is an intrusive medium. Products can be injected where they are not wanted—which doesn't sound very moral but which is a fact of life with television.

The last point is one which few people have articulated, at least to my satisfaction, and it is one which I personally feel is the most powerful thing television has going for it. Television is the medium which depends least on consumer cooperation to develop a rich response to symbolic stimulation. If you think about it for a minute, a printed page is nothing more than black marks on white paper until such time as a response is created in the reader. The printed page is a very abstract language. So is radio: it depends wholly on audio stimulation. Colored pictures are also very abstract. All media other than television are very limited. Television is the screen art. This is the medium which in effect *packages an experience* and brings the consumer into it. Television provides him with a response which he would otherwise have to contribute in a major part *out of himself*. For the low-interest products, where the consumer is not interested in responding to stimulation—products such as soaps, waxes, bug-killers and the like—television has provided the opportunity to make these dull things vital so that the consumer will respond. While this represents a selfish point of view, it has a very important implication for the intellectual field as well. With the advantages we have in television, we have what I call the Jekyll and Hyde implications. Television stimulates with its great selling force; it stimulates innovations, permitting us to introduce new products. But it also stimulates obsolescence, so we are in a product rat race because of television. At substantially increased costs it is going to be difficult to introduce these new products unless they are of a market-shaking dimension. Thus, the stimulus of television will in effect entrench the present products where they are now. As television becomes more fractionated in its audience appeal, it becomes less valuable as a mass medium. Obviously it then becomes less valuable to us and to the educators, as I will try to illustrate later.

Television has some product problems, one of which is the inevitability of mass program failures in a mass market concept. When the audience potential is limited and there is a failure to make an economic adjustment, it is a very bad thing for the advertiser, for the talent, and for the networks. Let me explain. The television potential for any given time period is limited, since during each year approximately the same number of homes will tune into a particular time period. You can't have all winners; either you have one failure or no winners. This is a fact of life. It seems a cruel fact for the people who are creating television. Failure to recognize it seems wasteful from an economic point of view. In some way, I would think, it could be faced

so that the total investment in that time period does not exceed audience potential. How this feat is to be accomplished I don't know.

With television taking a more active part in education, public life,
and politics, I personally think that there is an awful lot of duplication of programming. I don't want to see the same program on three
networks, I think this is a waste. I think we are offering the consumer
a choice that isn't necessary. I think duplication of programming
tends to inject a sense of economic inflation into the medium in its en-
tirety, for which we pay and for which, ultimately, the consumer pays
because the advertisers must obtain fair value. The duplication of
facilities for political purposes, for example, is more of a response to
political pressure than to a valid judgment of the requirements of the
public.

Now I can attack the intellectual world a little. I think they have it
coming to them. The intellectual world fights vehemently for free expression, even of the most publicly noxious, political, social, and
moral views; and I agree with them. However, they strive to protect
the public from what they consider to be the trivial, not only in television, but everywhere else. I think this is a gross inconsistency. Another gross inconsistency, in my opinion, is their failure to recognize
that in television's mass audience and with a high level of symbolic
communication, they have an opportunity to reach mankind for the
first time in history. Yet they seek to fractionate these mass audiences
by converting the medium to a limited communication of what they
call "better" programming, and what I call "non-mass" programming.

One last point about the chronic problems: we have what I call the
classic dilemma of convergence. At the same time that it becomes
more difficult to program fresh material at high levels of creativity,
consumer tastes are being raised. They are being raised by exposure
to television and its current programming. If entertainment has to be

in some way uncommon, that is, to provide what the viewer cannot get for himself first hand, how far can television go in being uncommon enough to engage the viewer without dooming itself as a mass medium? This is a problem for the future.

I would like to express a personal point of view about the direction of television; I'm speaking out as an advertiser and I'm also speaking as an intellectual. I think that television in the near future must remain essentially as it is today—virtually 100 per cent commercial and scarcely less dull to most of us—if it is to be truly a mass medium. I think it must remain a mass medium if it is to realize its potential as the most powerful means of cultural advancement that mankind has ever devised. To realize its cultural potential, it must evolve toward higher levels and richer content of communication at a pace acceptable to a mass public. I don't know how fast a pace is acceptable to a mass public. I do think that in order to evolve, television must change slowly from within and the plan of change must be sufficiently real to counter the pressures of the politically expedient and the intellectually irresponsible. We have a lot at stake in television and we hope that it will be advertisers and not Medicare which will support television in its later years. We plan to support the development of television as long as it is a good economic proposition for us, and for television also; but we expect the television industry to pursue good business practices, especially in the area of cost control. I think that television can be a mass medium as long as mass media are possible. But it must be a mass medium that evolves in harmony with its own influence on the public and does so in economic equilibrium with advertisers.

LEONARD S. MATTHEWS

The Advertising Agency

First of all, what does an advertising agency do? Well, just as the name says, we are agents for our clients. We operate in their behalf and for their benefit, and we are an extension of the total marketing efforts of the companies we serve. We serve them differently depending upon their marketing, their objectives, and their points of view. We are a collection of generalists and specialists who through combined science and art, attempt to create advertising communications to help sell the goods and services of our clients; and that is our basic and overriding objective.

We have an administration to manage our shop; we have general services to do the housekeeping of our business; we have research to tell us what's right and what's wrong about our advertising, to tell us about the markets we attempt to reach and penetrate—what consumer targets we seek—and to feed back measurements of the results of our efforts to improve and change our advertising. We have a function which might be called variously engineering or production in other businesses and this is, of course, our creative operation. In our company for example, we have over three hundred people directly involved in the preparation of ads and commercials—in the creative functions. This includes all the writers, artists, layout men, type experts, commercial-production experts, and film directors. These are people steeped in the knowledge of our clients' products and services and the facts of the market's prospects. They synthesize everything they know, suffuse it with imagination, sparkle it with brilliance, we hope, and finally make ads.

And of course these ads have to be placed. Once we have made these selling communications they must be distributed; the departments concerned with the distribution of these messages are what we call Media and Programming. The Media-Programming departments, working very closely with research, are involved in making sure that the "who, what, when, and where" of the placement of these commercial messages is properly handled. For example, last year we handled something like 3,385 different printed advertisements in 500 different newspapers and magazines, on about 350 different dates; 1,200 different television commercials scheduled into over 10,000 network television commercial positions and over 250,000 local television spots. And all this happens with no more than a fraction of 1 per cent error.

Finally we have the equivalent of a sales force, called Client Service. Client Service in our business, contrary to the conception of many outsiders, is not martinis and entertainment. It's the highly professional and increasingly scientific function of providing our clients with a totality of marketing. It means the pulling together of all the specialists in an agency to make sure they are all operating on the same track and for the same objectives as those of the client. Perhaps the greatest generalists in the complex, changing agency world are these Client Service people, or Account Executives, or Client Representatives.

Obviously, all of this has to be done on the basis of a blueprint, a strategy, a procedure, a tactic; this is very important in keeping all of these people working on the same track. Within the framework of, say, a 10 million dollar account, there may be some four hundred people in an agency over a period of a month who will work at some point, in some little way, on that account. If you try to combine their efforts without marketing strategy, without a basic approach, you get lost and you lose money. One of the things that these specialists might decide to use would be network television. They would decide the form of network to be used, and, within that form, on which particular programs to place client advertising. Such decisions would all be multiple-department operations.

No medium matches television's potency as a pervasive, involving medium; and if properly used it is an outstanding advertising tool. There are, of course, other advertising media that do certain jobs better than television, but television certainly has to be regarded as number one in effectiveness today for most products. Despite the critics of television, viewer consumption is at an all-time high. Six hours a day as most of you know is what Nielsen tells us the viewer is watching and there is no apparent development of apathy or rejection despite what we hear. However, there is the problem that television is not appealing equally to all segments of the public. Three-fourths of the viewing is done by 40 per cent of the viewers, and many people who are not viewing very much are excellent prospects for many things we sell, so we should learn more about them. The message is perishable, as we know; and this fact is another problem we should address ourselves to with increasing effort.

We can reach immense numbers of people once or many times with a commercial message, but the unit cost of commercials is increasing at a faster rate than audience growth. Until about two years ago, despite the fantastic increases in the cost of doing business in television, the audiences were growing. We have now reached relative maturity in that cost efficiencies are reducing, and those of us in the business of spending our clients' money are becoming a little concerned. Also the progressive commercialization of the medium is a problem. The high level of other nonprogram material, which in our judgment adulterates the commercial unit, is something that has to be watched.

We also think we ought to do a lot more about trying to find out how television affects *people* and not simply *homes*. Most of our audience measurements are on television homes and this is a relatively imprecise unit. We need to know more about how it affects people specifically.

There is a projected increase in the number of television outlets with the UHF stations growing very fast, CATV developing, and of course the possibility that pay TV is going to get approval from the FCC. At the same time there are no compensating cost reductions. These, along with the increasing costs of color, are matters we have to be concerned about. Program costs are piling up and no apparent effort is being made to alleviate them. The producers and the guilds apparently believe there is no bottom to the advertisers' budget, and this is absolutely not so. There is no evidence that broadcasters' historically unilateral and, at times, authoritarian behavior will change. Broadcasters sometimes, but not often enough, consult the advertising agencies before making sweeping and costly changes in policies and practices. We think, too, that sometimes there is an unthinking elimination of profitable advertising benefits which cost the networks nothing. Billboards and such are eliminated when there is no apparent need to eliminate them.

We are also concerned about the responsibilities which various groups who make up this medium have to the public. We know what the government's responsibility is. We think the broadcasters have a responsibility to provide reasonably balanced program schedules, to offer the viewers a choice, to attempt to raise the viewers' standards of appreciation, to innovate and exercise the public's consciousness and its mental muscles, to be involved in community problems, and to provide the advertisers with a reasonable audience circulation at reasonable costs. Advertisers, too, have a responsibility to use television as more than a distributor of commercial messages and to employ its power in the public interest as well as in their private interest, to provide more honest commercials, and to pay fair prices for a fair value. We think viewers have a responsibility also—to be active and vocal, and to react to good as well as bad television.

We think that television is a business—profit-intended and profit-motivated. The power of television makes the responsibility of the broadcasters vital. Even so, television is not a public service and, in our view, it does not have to provide programming for every single intellectual splinter of our population. As a business, television cannot avoid its interbusiness responsibility of providing a fair return not only to its investors and itself, but to its users as well.

Now let's take a look into the future. The French say "the more things change, the more they are the same." We say, "the only thing that is constant is change." When it comes to television, looking back at its fifteen-year-plus history and ahead into its geometrically changing future, we might say whatever can change will change. The changes, which are in the best interest of our society and our economy, are perhaps more likely to become reality if, to the degree that we influence our business environment, we put our weight behind them. Television is a splendid marketing tool, but we have every expectation that over the years it can become more and more powerful, more and more precise, and more and more effective.

Here is a list of some evolutionary, or perhaps revolutionary, changes that could happen in television's accelerating and expanding future. Research will become more and more essential. It is terribly important to find out what television does to people and how they react. Why do people watch one program and not another? What emotional satisfactions do they seek in television, and which of these are fulfilled? Could certain new program types attract light or non-viewers to television? We could ask a hundred more questions, but the basic point is that when we know more about what's happening to the audience and why, we will be able to employ television as a more effective marketing tool. I predict that creative people will fashion new programs that will select the viewers, in contrast to the present gross method in which the viewer selects the program.

It seems inevitable that the costs of television will continue to increase and it seems likely that the rate of increase, as contrasted with more recent years, may accelerate. I hope not. Even at present audiences are not increasing at a rate comparable to the rising costs. At the same time the number of available television channels is increasing. This means more slices to the pie. The result is that in all probability the "individual per brand" use of television as a marketing tool will change in size and shape. Many brands that can afford national television now probably won't be able to afford it in the future. The use of national television will perhaps be reduced.

The forms and patterns of commercials may change. We now have a gallery of commercial forms, as well as the commercial insertion patterns borrowed from radio. Does this have to be? We range from an 8-second ID to a 60-second commercial. The limited possibilities of commercial formats and present commercial time allowance may be too confining as costs increase and as audiences are fractionalized and become more selective. There is no "black magic" that says everything has to be as it is now. Maybe we should think in terms of new commercial rates and new commercial scheduling patterns which would fit the television of the future better than the present arrangements do.

Some people believe that blocks of commercial time will be developed as is done in some places in South America and in some European television. Interestingly enough, I am told that some of these 15-minute blocks of uninterrupted commercials, back-to-back, are among the highest-rated programs on those stations. While some people believe that television would be improved by this system, I'm not one of them.

I am concerned with the increase in total commercial time and deeply concerned that we haven't seen the end of that rising curve. On daytime television 24 per cent of the time is commercial at the moment. About 13 per cent of prime time is commercial. This compares pretty favorably with print media. We estimate that about 25 per cent is the figure in radio, about 60 per cent in newspapers, and 45 to 50 per cent in consumer magazines. These kinds of commercial densities would probably be very unattractive in television because television is more demanding from the audience's point of view. I'm not making a value judgment, I'm describing what exists and the changes that are taking place.

I think a couple of things will or should happen as these developments take place. We must learn more about commercials so that, although our advertising may be more in evidence, it will be more pleasant and more persuasive. We must also learn more about the placement of commercials, so that they are not lost in this increased commercial time and that the end result will not be like an animated classified newspaper page.

As costs increase and audiences are fractionalized there will, in all likelihood, follow a redirection of substantial portions of national advertising budgets toward more selected use of television advertising. This perhaps will lead to more program services than we have today. Essentially we have three program services represented by our major television networks. As we see the audience more fragmented and more selective we will see more local program services, more regional services, and perhaps even more than three national network services. Satellites of course also bring forward the possibility of a more selective distribution system. Specialized stations may develop. As surely as consumer print magazines can support a range of publications from *Mad Magazine* to *Scientific American*, doesn't it seem possible that television as it matures could develop a broader range of stations serving a variety of needs? We could see the birth and growth of a television equivalent of *Parents' Magazine* and *Woman's Day* and *House Beautiful*. Such a change would be very interesting to advertisers and agencies who are trying to sell products to specific customers. Such specialized programming could select its audiences with considerable accuracy.

Another possibility would be a television channel that played fine classical music and illustrated it with appropriate mood photography. This is not something of wide audience appeal, but could very well find its place in the television of tomorrow. The all-news station could evolve: not the kind of CATV station which runs a teletype on camera, but a genuine all-news station. This could have an appeal to the advertiser and provide a very good service for the viewer.

A creative revolution will be brought on by rising costs. We must find ways to make television more productive. The myth of complete price elasticity as far as the advertiser is concerned has got to be slain because many advertisers are running out of money in terms of the efficient use of television for specific brands. So with the number of television stations perhaps doubling in a decade and all of these new program services, the pie will be sliced up in many little pieces. The challenge to the creative people is obvious. The audience is going to turn off its sets if it is fed the 109th re-run of *I Love Lucy* or if the *Sands of Iwo Jima* is run for the 25th time, even if it is run backwards and the Japanese are allowed to win. We need to look for undiscovered and unplumbed creative sources. The independent program producers and the networks are turning now to this problem. The big revolution in television is going to come in the creative area. Whole new concepts of programming will have to appear.

Still another possibility is stay-at-home shopping by television. This marketing phenomenon is near at hand for even now it is technically feasible. Multiple channels can be received and the signal can be scrambled so certain homes can't receive it. Banks right now are working on a universal dialed credit card system. It's possible to put merchandise on a television channel and have a shopper at home view both the merchandise and the price information, then dial the number, have the merchandise shipped out to her home and have it billed through her bank credit system. All of that technology is available for use today. Should this development take place, it does not seem unreasonable that some kinds of advertising will actually decline. The merchandise will have to be brought to that shopping channel pre-sold. The buyer won't be exposed to point-of-purchase material or to personal salesmanship in some kinds of merchandise. A new kind of advertising may become more important. It could be that the manufacturer may become his own retailer and ship the merchandise directly from regional warehouses. Television could change the traditional patterns of the retail merchandising.

With a television system that is wired and national we could evolve the ultimate in distribution of commercial messages by 1984. Family purchase patterns, rates, and brand profiles for all products would be automatically tabulated with any and every purchase and this information would be programmed and available to an advertiser for a fee. In turn an advertising campaign using perhaps entirely different commercials might be beamed to each group of prospects depending upon their use of the product. We might allot 10 per cent of our advertising dollar to the lowest quintile and 35 per cent to the highest quintile. We would be paid for our advertising in direct proportion to the number of customers exposed to the advertising message. The instant coffee population, for example, would be known. We could locate these people and we would know specifically what television programs would reach them and we would charge on the basis of our specific market delivery.

We see many changes ahead in television. We've conjectured some ways in which television may change. We hope the changes that do occur will be those brought about through the combined creativity and logical planning of those of us in the businesses of marketing and communication.

THOMAS MOORE

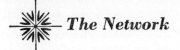 *The Network*

First, a network is not licensed by the government. All three networks own and operate stations in five of the major markets in the country and these stations are licensed. But the government itself is not a check against networks directly: rather it is a check of owned and operated stations. I think it is important to realize that networks came into being out of a need on the part of the stations. The necessity for a unified collective programming organization and for a unified sales and administrative organization brought the networks into being in radio and has carried over into television.

The regulation that grants a station a license under the original Communication Act makes television first of all a business. It is, in my opinion, a good thing that the television system we have has grown out of free enterprise. I think it's tragic that a few people in recent days have been tempted to divide our industry into what they call professionals and what they call managers. There is no such division and any effort to make one is wrong and is doing a disservice to the industry. There are responsible managing professionals in our business, the classification to which we all think we belong, and certainly there are managing professionals and professional managers.

The right of profit should not be put in a defensive position as it has in some academic discussions of television today. I dare say no one can prove that television would have advanced to the point it has today had there not been the free enterprise system. One need only to look at the French and the Italian systems, which are a few years younger than the American system, to realize the difference that can be brought about through the so-called commercialism.

I think that networks through their stations have developed a keen sense of responsibility, first of all, to the viewing public, because without the public we cannot compete and we cannot survive. And I think competition for audiences has been a healthy thing for television even though it is now referred to as the "numbers' game." That is not to say that I don't believe the "numbers' game" has been greatly abused. Our responsibility extends directly through the audience to the advertisers and the advertising agencies. There is also a third factor and it must be faced squarely, and this is that we have a responsibility to stockholders. These responsibilities must all be met within the framework of a commercial operation.

Now, in the development of television networks as we know them, many problems have appeared. These problems are in the process of being solved—some too slowly. Others seem frustrating and impossible, yet there must be, somewhere along the way, solutions. We all know the history of the VHF-UHF problem. There is a tremendous difference in the reach of each network—actually CBS and NBC are very high—and we at ABC still have a marked deficiency even though the UHF, which is coming along fairly well, is going to serve to alleviate a good portion of that inefficiency.

There is the other problem of the cost factor that has been forced upon all of us by the competitive system. Color, full color programming at least at night—and before another year and a half or two years everything on television will, of course, be in color—has added to costs. Our one network alone must spend 18.5 million dollars more in order to program in color, from September through the first twenty-six weeks of the coming season, the same number of hours as formerly were programmed in black and white. A great deal of that results from inflationary costs in general, but a good portion of it is the added cost of color. This figure is an example of some of the spiralling costs about which the advertiser and advertising agency are concerned.

Another serious problem for all networks is that none of us is operating at a top program efficiency. Perhaps we are programming too much time for the Ada, Oklahomas, as well as for the Philadelphias, and for the Bostons. Each of the networks ends up programming some twenty-four hours at night between 7:30 and 11:00 in full color in direct competition with similar programming by the other networks. The result is that, with possibly one or two minor exceptions, in no single market except network owned and operated stations do all of those programs appear in the time period, nor do they appear at all in many areas. These are some of the severe hurdles that our business must overcome in the next few years. But overcome them I'm sure that we will.

Certainly we all know that television can be better. But we all know also that it is better today than yesterday—and it was better yesterday than a year ago. If you doubt that, just go back and look at some of the programs in the past and measure the differences in the general television fare and in scheduling of public affairs and nonfiction between what exists today and what existed at that time. One thing that's going to develop out of the coming seasons is a new competition for quality among the networks. I will be the first to admit that competition has been far too strenuous in the area of rating points, in the area of dollars, and in the area of nonprestige programming. We can now begin to compete for some of the things that might be available to us if we go out and search.

Competition among the three networks has been very hearty and brisk and rough. No holds have been barred. And I don't think there is much chance that competition for quality will change in the least the financial aspects of the competition for entertainment programming and for audiences. Historically, whenever the ABC has entered a somewhat different arena, the competition has become pretty strenuous for that category of programming. I'm certainly referring now to 1956 and 1957 when we started battling on action programming. The competition got pretty rough and the viewer got some good action programs. In 1960 when we decided to build the sports operation and we got into the field suddenly, one thing happened—the costs went sky high. The truth of the matter is that as three competing networks we were all able to improve, and no single area in television has come closer to fulfilling its promise than has the area of sports. Likewise, all of us followed NBC's lead of many, many years ago in pre-empting programming freely when we really believed that we could offer a better program than the straight "good guy, bad guy" kind of show. I know that we are running into CBS and we are running into NBC in our quest for quality with our ABC *Stage '67*. I'm sure that competition is going to get more heated. But I was never so sure of anything in my life as I am that television will improve, will become greater, and will become better through a fully competitive and a fully free enterprise system. We at ABC intend to be right in the thick of it.

DISCUSSION

"Television from the Inside" by the four panelists gave the conferees the kinds of presentations to which they were most accustomed. These were clear explanations of the functions of each of the areas touching television and expressions of some hope for the future. In every case the speaker made the point that he was engaged in a business. This is well because although the professional may have difficulty remembering that he is not simply in business, but that he is in the business of communication, the educator and the nonprofessional have difficulty remembering that the communicators in the various areas of television are also businessmen.

The discussion at the main session was reinforced in the group meetings on several issues. One was the matter of rising costs. As more than one speaker pointed out, the disproportionate rise in costs is due to color television, to inflationary trends, and to rising demands from talent and workers connected with the business. Rising costs can be managed if profits rise correspondingly. If this does not happen in at least one or more of the areas impinging on television, the problem becomes serious. Network television has been so costly for many years that only a limited number of national advertisers can afford the medium. If costs continue to escalate, even some of the present advertisers may turn to other media to advertise their products. It was brought out that television inherited its methods of advertising and business from radio and perhaps different methods and approaches should be investigated.

There was considerable discussion concerning the number of commercials and their placement. A major difficulty, directly caused by rising costs, is the addition of local commercials during station breaks. In reality, no more time is devoted to commercials than was the case a few years ago. The viewer, however, sees more and shorter commercials in the same time allotments. There has also been an increase in nonprogram, noncommercial material such as credits, billboards, piggy-backs, and such. Effort should be made to reduce the amount of noncreative material drawing attention from the commercial messages which must pay for the program. The suggestion of placing commercials one after another in a single block drew fire. There has been no satisfactory research as to the relative effectiveness of block commercials as opposed to the conventional methods; but block commercials were, in general, considered less effective in selling individual products.

The placement of commercials, especially in dramatic programs, presents a critical problem for producers. This is particularly true in movies which were not planned for television and have no breaks written into the dramatic action. The difficulty is further increased by the tendency to increase the number of interruptions during the last hour of the film. The issue came up again in relation to news programs, where the commercial may not be compatible with serious news. Awareness of the difficulties of commercial placement is an important first step, but the final solution to these problems will be more difficult to reach.

Each of the speakers, in one way or another, expressed both the hope and the desire for improved television. These feelings were expressed rather tentatively, for no one really wished to voice his misgivings. As the discussions continued, though, it became apparent that the consensus was that television, while better than in the past, was not what it could or ought to be. When there was tacit agreement to this position, the question turned on just what specific action was feasible.

Indeed, if it could be said that the balance of the Seminar rested on a single fulcrum, it would have been this.

The dilemma as expressed in group sessions, from the platform, and in general discussion was this: assuming that television could be better, how was it to be made better without destroying its wide appeal? The dilemma stated in its extreme is quite clear. If television were suddenly changed to satisfy the needs of the elite, television would no longer be a means of mass communication. It is doubtful if it would be anything, because the elite, despite their criticism, are not really viewers of television anyway, and they have at their command other ample means to satisfy their intellectual, cultural, and entertainment needs. If the dilemma is not stated in the extreme, the impossible choices may not appear to be so disastrous. Could television lead the tastes of the public rather than reflect these tastes? This question and the several corollary questions were raised again and again in the several general and group meetings.

TELEVISION: THE BROAD VIEW

DAVID POTTER

The Historical Perspective

The subject of television in America, viewed broadly, is tempting because it invites us to write our own ticket. I would like, therefore, to say at the outset that it is treacherous because it invites us to speculate in futures. When we speculate in futures, there are two ways we can do it. One way is simply to let the imagination off the leash and to try to picture what would be the ideal conditions of an optimum world. In such a world, of course, every television program would be as good as another Fifth Symphony or another Gettysburg Address. Every audience would want only programs of the highest absolute merit, and every sponsor and broadcaster would want only to give it to them. But I will refrain from filling out the details of this seductive and utopian picture.

The other way to speculate in futures is to define what are the controlling conditions in a situation, and to ask realistically and analytically in what ways these conditions may be expected to change. It is this kind of speculation in which I shall engage. Being an historian, I am not troubled by looking backward at where I have been as a means of seeing where I am going. It seems to me that three conditions have shaped the structure and determined the character of American television. The first of these is a technical condition, namely that the number of available channels has been very few and the possible variety of programs which could be offered simultaneously has, therefore, been very small. The second is an economic condition, namely that the financial basis of television has been advertising, and this has meant that a great system of public communication was financed by payments from producers who were not concerned primarily with public communication but with the sale of whatever it is that they happen to produce. The third is a social condition, namely that the audience for American television is what may be called a mass society which has somewhat different values and social controls from the traditional western society. In the traditional society, the upper classes set the standards of the culture and the lower classes followed along with these standards as best they could. Sometimes they had a subculture, which we call a folk culture, of their own but they did not challenge nor resist the standards of the elite.

All these conditions have been brought to bear upon television in a very brief time historically. It is hard, today, to remember or even to believe that as recently as twenty-seven years ago, only a handful of Americans had ever seen a visual image broadcast over the air. Then, in 1939, at the New York World's Fair, millions of people saw television for the first time, and Dumont started selling home television receivers. But for another decade, television developed relatively slowly. Technical problems of coordinating the specifications of receivers with the intended specifications of broadcasting delayed rapid development, as did the priorities of a war economy. As recently as eighteen years ago—can you believe it?—there were still only seventeen stations on the air and only eight cities with television service.

To say this is to say that since 1948, television has developed with such gigantic and rapid strides that it was almost impossible to grasp the magnitude of what was happening. Television overthrew the ascendancy of radio, after radio had been a dominant form of communication for scarcely twenty years. Television emptied the motion picture theaters and appeared likely to bankrupt the motion picture producers until they discovered that they could sell their accumulated backlogs of films to television broadcasters and could profit by producing for the television industry as they had once profited by producing for the customers at the box office. Today it appears that the production of motion pictures is, in the broad sense, almost a subsidiary of television.

Having clearly reduced the motion picture and radio to subordinate roles, television now shares domination of the field of public communication with only one other medium—the printed medium of newspapers, magazines, and books. This sharing is not equal in a qualitative sense, for the printed page has certain informational, educational, and artistic functions which television, at present, lacks. Most of all, the printed medium has permanence and can be preserved and consulted repeatedly, while the images that come over the air waves are transitory or momentary. Moreover, printed materials can offer infinite choice to various readers simultaneously, while television as yet offers a limited range of programs, which tend to incorporate common denominators for the mass audience rather than to provide diversity for varied audiences. But despite these qualitative differences, the quantitative fact remains that the American people spend more time looking at television screens than they spend looking at print. Their consumption of television drama vastly exceeds their consumption of fiction. Their information on public affairs may still be gained primarily from newspapers and magazines, but visual images and spoken messages have an immediacy which the printed word lacks, and whatever strong opinions or feelings of urgency people may feel about public questions are likely to be shaped more by news broadcasts and documentaries than by news dispatches and editorials. Also, it is well to remember that television reaches millions of viewers who have no access to the printed page, and these viewers are at an especially formative stage in their lives, for they are the children who are too young to read.

When we speak, then, of the history of American television, we are speaking of the history of a dominant form of public communication in the United States. Americans sit in the dark for no one really knows how many hundreds of millions of hours per night in front of the screens on which the pictures are projected. Television has become a major element in American life, and many travellers who eighteen years ago had never seen a television set today will not stay in a motel room overnight unless they are provided with one.

Everyone today can recognize the predominant and universal place which television has come to occupy, but the basic conditions which have shaped the character of television in America, and which I have attempted to define, are much less easy either to recognize or to understand. The implications of a mass society are not easily spelled out. Even more, the ambiguity of television's relationship with advertising almost unavoidably invites confusion. Looking first at the advertising side, and then at the communications side of the television coin, one asks is this primarily a medium of public entertainment which happens to be supported financially by advertising, or is it primarily an apparatus for the marketing of consumer goods which uses public communications as part of the marketing process? The planners of programs for American viewers are also, to some extent, the planners of sales for American producers. The public is an audience, but it is also a market. It could not be a market unless it had given its consent to be an audience, and it could not remain an audience, in the present context, unless it had proved itself as a market. Historical circumstances have created an anomalous situation which logic could never produce. The financial support which shapes the programs of the millions is not provided by a Bureau of Culture which decides what people shall look at, nor by a pay-as-you-watch system which permits the spectator to support his own preferences with his own financial support; it is provided instead by the makers of automobiles, detergents, cigarettes, depilatories, packaged foods, headache remedies, shampoos. The point here is not that there is anything inherently wrong with depilatories, any more than there is with less-intimate products, but only that the makers of depilatories have no special competence for the role which history has whimsically assigned to them as arbiters of American entertainment and shapers of policy in the field of public communications. An old saying affirms that he who pays the piper shall call the tune, or as an historian would state it, no power exceeds the power of the purse. The purse for the programs which divert the American people is held by parties who care nothing about the diversion for its own sake, but care a great deal about whether the diversion can sell tobacco, or aspirin, or cake-mix.

When I say this, it is not a signal that I mean to launch into a well-worn academic diatribe against television. What I personally believe about television is only what many broadcasters believe with more intense feeling than I. I do believe that television falls distressingly short of fulfilling its social potentialities and that it gives little of the nourishment to the human spirit which a great and vital medium of communication can give and ought to give. But I also believe it is unrealistic to be shocked when an advertising medium resorts to advertising practices. Men who live by advertising must sell, just as men who live by soldiering must fight and men who live by politics must make compromises. A person who wants to understand soldiering, or politics, or television will not do so by attributing the shortcomings of the system to the personal qualities of the men involved in it. Instead, he will examine the dynamics of the system itself, and if he does this with television, it will bring him quickly back to the technical and economic and social determinants which I have mentioned.

If we examine these determinants with any care, we will soon see that television, like many another force in history, developed in a way which no one really foresaw. Technically, of course, television is sim-

ply a method of broadcasting pictures over the air waves in a fashion
not basically different from the way in which radio can broadcast
sounds. Because of this fact, the shaping of the structure of radio communication predetermined much of the structure of television communication; and, like many another infant, television came into the
world to meet a destiny which had been fixed before it was born.

Radio, of course, began as something vastly different from what it
became. It started as a system of sending telegraphic messages by code
without wires. An individual sender transmitted a message which was
intended to be picked up by an individual receiver. As early as 1916,
some people, including David Sarnoff, saw that there was more to it
than this, and Sarnoff wrote a memorandum saying, "I have in mind
a plan of development which would make radio a 'household utility'
in the same sense as the piano or phonograph. The idea is to bring
music into the house by wireless . . . The receiver can be designed in
the form of a simple Radio Music Box and arranged for several dif-
erent wave lengths."

But Sarnoff was ahead of his time. Most people, including Congressmen and federal officials, thought of radio mostly as a device for
sending messages to and from ships at sea. During World War I, the
government took over control of the air waves and vested this control
in the Navy Department. In 1919, when Lee De Forest was experi-
menting with informal broadcasts of phonograph records, a government radio inspector forced him off the air with the immortal assurance that "There is no room in the ether for entertainment."

In 1918 the Alexander Bill was introduced in Congress to place
radio under government control, but Congressman Alexander had no
concept of radio as a medium of mass communication, and there was
never any serious effort in this country to establish government operation or even close control of the air waves. It is true that the government asserted in the Radio Act of 1927 that the air waves belonged to

the people; and it is true also that ever since the decision of the Supreme Court in the case of *Munn v. Illinois* in 1876, the principle had been recognized that business, which was "affected with the public interest," was subject to government regulation. But at a more pragmatic level, the American tradition had placed strong taboos upon government activity in any area which could be occupied by private enterprise, and public property had been thrown open, as far as possible, to private use. The great ranchers had been permitted to graze their cattle on the open range of the public domain; the great mining companies had been permitted to stake their bonanza claims on government land at a minimum of expense. Even when the government wanted a transcontinental railroad badly enough to pay the costs of building it, it extended loans and gave gifts of public land to the privately owned Central Pacific and Union Pacific Railroads to enable them to pay the costs of construction. As a Congressman at the time stated the situation, "the government in fact builds the road and ought to control and own it." But the basic reality was that the American people did not want the government to operate a railroad if it could be owned privately. This attitude remained dominant, and it extended to the fact that the public did not even favor very much regulation. When railroad abuses became serious, some regulatory power was vested in the Interstate Commerce Commission, and during the administration of Theodore Roosevelt this power was actually made substantial. But on the whole, regulation went against the American grain, and the fact that the air waves belonged to the public carried no necessary implication that the use of the air waves would be vigorously regulated.

The fact is that governmental operation or even positive public control of the air channels was never a practicable alternative or even a live issue in the United States. This fact was made abundantly clear by the Radio Act of 1927 and by the Communication Act of 1934, which were more important for what they did not enact than for what they did. Under these pieces of legislation, first a Federal Radio Commission and later a Federal Communications Commission were created, with responsibility for licensing broadcast stations and for insisting that a certain proportion of the time of a station should be devoted to sustaining programs or to programs in the public interest. But once these requirements were met, somewhat mechanically, the Commission had little actual voice in the nature of the programming. The Supreme Court stated the realities rather clearly when it said, "Congress intended to leave competition in the business of broadcasting where it found it, to permit a licensee who was not interfering electrically with other broadcasters to survive or succumb according to his ability to make his programs attractive to the public." Thus, the chief public responsibility of a broadcaster in the eyes of Congress was to avoid interfering electrically with another broadcaster.

Even when it became clear—if indeed it had ever been in doubt— that the control of the air waves would be left to private enterprise, there was still a great deal of uncertainty as to what form of private enterprise might take hold. The costs of early broadcasting, which often consisted merely of playing phonograph records over the air, were low, and the manufacturers of radio receiving sets and equipment tended to suppose that they would pay these costs out of revenue from the sale of radios. There was some discussion, mostly quite vague, of financial support from public subscription, or from endowment, or from taxes on receiving sets. At the outset the prospect that advertising might become the financial mainstay of the broadcasting industry was but dimly perceived, and was often rejected insofar as it was perceived. Broadcasting was not visualized as a direct profit-making venture. Thus in 1922, when David Sarnoff proposed setting up a network company, he wrote, "I feel that, with suitable publicity activities, such a company will ultimately be regarded as a public institution of great

value in the same sense that a library, for example, is regarded."
When General James G. Harbord, president of RCA, offered the vice-
presidency of the corporation to George F. McClelland, McClelland
asked how commercial the venture was to be. Harbord reassured him
that ". . . we had the ambition to give a splendid public service, not
unconscious of the fact, however, that if we did it, it would reflect itself to us in profits by that company and increased sales of radio apparatus by our own." Sydney Head in his excellent study *Broadcasting in
America* says that when the first Radio Conference met at Washington
in 1922, the sentiment against advertising "was almost universal."
Even as late as the fourth conference in 1925, when advertising was
beginning to be accepted, the committee on advertising and publicity
declared that direct advertising was objectionable, and it reported in
favor of good-will advertising only. This attitude lingered as late as
1929, when "direct" advertising was still supposed to be limited to
daylight hours, while evening programs were to be punctuated only
by a dignified identification of sponsors.

Yet, as broadcasting grew, broadcasters inevitably discovered an inescapable truth: the readiest source of revenue, and perhaps the only
really practicable source, was advertising. Heavy endowment was not
forthcoming and the manufacturers of receiving sets did not have a
real incentive to pay the costs of the expensive programs which the
public soon grew to expect. The broadcasters really had nothing to
sell except access to a mass audience, and the only parties who had
reason to pay for such access were advertisers. In 1922 station WEAF
stumbled upon this axiomatic reality—the most far-reaching inadver-
tent discovery since Columbus encountered the Americas as unsus-
pected obstacles in his path westward to the Indies. Sydney Head
states that Gimbel Brothers, using WEAF, was the first commercial
advertiser known to have provided entertainment along with the commercial, thus treating the listeners simultaneously as both audience

and market. It is for this, and not for its merchandising, that Gimbel's
ought to be remembered in history.

Once the marriage of broadcasting and advertising took place, it led
over a straight road from which there were no turnoffs to the historical anomaly which I mentioned earlier, namely that a vital influence
in public communications is exercised by large companies which neither aspired to nor claimed qualifications in this field. This conjunc-
tion of advertising and programming is one of the decisive historical
factors which have shaped the character of American television.

A great deal has been said by a great many people about the effects
of advertising upon television. I have said some of it myself in a little
book entitled *People of Plenty*. Critics who idealize democracy are
loath to admit that the public may prefer mediocre programs to programs of merit. Hence they often approach this question with the belief that when public standards are poor, they must have been sub-
verted by the media, the advertisers, or some other external influence.
Implicitly, they assume that advertising imposes a low standard of
taste. This may be good democratic dogma, but the real trouble with
advertising is something quite different: the trouble is that it does not
impose any standard at all, high or low. It goes with the mass public,
up or down, and leaves the medium at the mercy of majority standards, whatever these standards may happen to be. In a society with
high cultural standards very widely held, advertising would almost
automatically adapt itself to those standards. But the evidence is, in
fact, fairly clear that the popular standards of the mass society are not
high, and the record is full of examples of motion pictures, television
programs, and other productions of merit which were snubbed by the
mass public. Leo Rosten has stated the case very pungently in saying,
"When the public is free to choose among various products, it chooses
—again and again and again—the frivolous against the serious, 'escape' as against reality, the lurid as against the tragic, the trivial as

against the serious, fiction as against fact, the diverting as against the significant."

Certainly there is a measure of truth in this indictment. It is impressive to note, as Yale Roe points out in *The Television Dilemma*, that when broadcasters are confronted with demands for public-service programming, they may be reluctant to put this programming at prime hours, but their most acute anxiety centers about offering a program of merit when a competing broadcaster is offering a program of pure fantasy or diversion. They know that the program of merit will suffer. It is also, I think, impressive to note that many of the criticisms of television programming—criticisms of the banality, the failure to depict life as it is, the lack of creative merit, the emphasis on the sadistic, the sensational, and the sordid—are applicable to branches of the mass media in which advertising plays a much smaller part than in television, or indeed in which advertising is lacking altogether. These criticisms are applicable, for instance, to the tabloid newspapers like the *New York Daily News* and the old *New York Mirror*; applicable for most of the drugstore paperback fiction, which contains no advertising; and applicable to popular motion pictures, which also contain no advertising and which were the objects of severe and justified criticism before television ever came on the scene or on the screen.

When I say that we may have attributed to advertising too specifically some of the evils inherent in the basic process of trying to reach a mass audience, I do not mean than we should simply relax and accept whatever level of programming or of popular taste happens to prevail. But I do mean that we need to recognize realistically some of the qualities of the mass society and some of the diversity of conditions which govern the various media in communicating with the mass society. When newspapers confronted this need, they responded to it, as all students of journalism know, by enlarging the range of their features, and offering something for everyone: a woman's page with household hints and advice to the lovelorn; a sports page for those who were fond of baseball, football, or betting, as the case might be; and a page of comic strips for the immature of all ages. Thus, the greater flexibility of the printed medium made it possible for the newspapers to try to attract everyone, without being forced to rely on one single common feature to accomplish this purpose. But the movies and television could not enlarge their audience by diversification, for they could not present several shows simultaneously, as a newspaper could. Instead, they were obliged to resort to a device which is artistically far more restrictive and stultifying—namely the fabrication of films or programs pitched at a level low enough to leave no one out, and confined to themes to which everyone will respond. These themes are few; they are emotional rather than intellectual; and they focus heavily upon sensation in the form either of sex or of violence. As Walter Lippmann pointed out many years ago, the minds of men vary more than their emotions, and if the attitudes of a large number of men are to be made uniform, if "one general will is to be forged out of a multiplicity of individual wishes," it must be done by "the use of symbols which assemble emotions after they have been detached from their ideas. The process, therefore, by which general opinions are brought to cooperation consists of an intensification of feeling and a degradation of significance."

The necessity to make one program attractive to everyone is indeed a limiting form of universalism. It dictates that the program cannot deal with topics of specialized interest, for fear of losing the attention of those who are indifferent to the topic; it cannot deal with topics at a mature level, for fear of losing the immature; and it cannot deal with anything controversial, for fear of antagonizing a portion of the audience. All this would be true even if the audience consisted of educated and intellectually responsible people. But the mass society which has formed the audience for American television has been neither highly educated nor intellectually eager.

To appreciate fully the controlling effect of the mass society upon television, it is perhaps necessary to try to imagine the difference that one might find between television as we know it and television as it might have been in a traditional society—for instance in the society of Victorian England or of Imperial Japan. In these and other traditional societies popular taste, as we call it, had little chance to develop or define itself. The public accepted standards of taste which were imposed by authority from above, and it imitated these standards. For instance, the bastard Gothic railroad stations of Victorian England, or the over-heated romances of the novelist Ouida, dealing with intense love affairs between superb guardsmen and females of sensibility, were examples of the adaptation of elite standards to the popular taste. The acutely class-conscious lower middle class zealously followed the standards of taste of the upper classes. Authority prevailed in matters of taste, as in political leadership, where the public voluntarily accepted the arrangement that high office should be held only by persons who were gentlemen born. If television had existed in the Victorian world, it would probably have adopted some sort of watered-down version of the taste that prevailed in the stately homes of England. Moreover, it would have encountered a socioeconomic structure in which a large part of the population lived at a subsistence level and could not have participated effectively as consumers in the mass market upon which television, as we know it today, is built.

In the United States, however, one of the basic facts, for good or ill, has been the repudiation of the principle of authority, and more particularly, the denial of any special ascendancy by the upper class. The War of Independence overthrew royal control and drove the Tories, who, by and large, were the gentlemen, out of the country. The advent of Jacksonian democracy established the proposition, for public purposes at least, that an uneducated backwoodsman was as good as a Harvard-bred gentleman, if not better. Ever since the time of Jackson, political candidates have stressed their humble origins—their log-cabin birth and their folksy qualities—rather than their qualifications of training and ability. Intellectualism was identified with the upper classes and with authority. Therefore there was a profound reaction against and distrust of intellectuals or, as they came to be called, "eggheads." Authority sold at such a heavy discount that Webster's dictionary, which unscrupulously advertises itself as an authority, adopted the view that even a sloppy and inferior word usage is "correct" if the abuse is committed by a large enough number of people. When authority went under a cloud, the standards which were upheld by authority went under a cloud also.

The American rejection of standards, because standards were identified with authority, is a vast and tempting subject, and it is one of the most crucial aspects of the social world into which American television was born. The theme would lend itself to lengthy development, but I must confine myself to two observations here: first that Alexis de Tocqueville made his classic diagnosis of the effect of democracy in producing mediocre standards of taste—made this diagnosis a full century before television was ever dreamed of; second, that Richard Hofstadter, in his *Anti-Intellectualism in American Life*, has assembled an immense amount of evidence of the distrust of excellence, and I might say the preference for mediocrity, which has prevailed historically in American society.

As the society grew, as urban centers proliferated, as an ill-assimilated and numerous population of immigrants who had been at the bottom of the scale in Europe, was added to the society, even the old community standards of the folk society in both Europe and America also began to give way. The mass society, as it is termed, began clearly to take the center of the stage. It is a basic fact of life that American television has served this mass society and has perhaps catered to some of its less fortunate qualities.

In this discussion I have tried to emphasize two factors which may seem to some extent to be contradictory. First, I have stressed what I believe to be the importance of advertising as a controlling factor in the programming of American television. This part of my discussion might seem to imply that the broadcasters and sponsors are responsible for whatever may be wrong. Second, I have emphasized the importance of a mass society which, in its tastes, has historically demonstrated a preference for the inferior. This might seem to imply that the public itself is responsible for inferior programs on the air waves and that the broadcasters and sponsors are merely innocent bystanders. But perhaps neither of these implications is valid. Perhaps the real point is that the centrality of advertising, along with the severe limitation in the number of channels, accentuated and, as it were, consummated television's dependence not only upon the mass audience, but upon the *average* level of the mass audience.

Even without advertising, we must suppose that the mass society would show in the realm of television the same preferences which it has shown in motion pictures, drugstore paperback fiction, and tabloid newspapers. For this reason, it seems historically unrealistic to suppose that television for the mass society could have been set at a fundamentally different standard even if the structure of control had been different. Critics who believe that pay television would achieve a high and consistent level of excellence ignore the fact that pay moving pictures have not done so. Critics who believe that vigorous public regulation alone could transform the quality of television forget that democratic public regulation would gravitate politically to the level of the mass society, just as market-oriented programming also gravitates economically toward the level of the mass society.

In following my historical factors, somewhat reluctantly, to these conclusions, let me say that I do not at all mean to suggest that television programming could not benefit by more vigorous regulation in certain respects, if only to prevent the more enlightened broadcasters from being victimized by the less enlightened. I certainly do not mean to suggest that the inferior standards of the mass society should stand as an excuse for the indifference to standards on the part of broadcasters. Least of all do I mean to rejoice that everything is for the best in this best of all possible television worlds.

But where does this lead in terms of my speculation in futures? It leads, I believe, to some conclusions about what it is realistic to expect in the way of improvement in television and what it is not realistic to expect. It is not realistic, I believe, to expect television or any other institution to operate at a level fundamentally different from the level of the mass society. As Richard Hofstadter has shown, when American society was anti-intellectual, even American education became anti-intellectual. It is not realistic, moreover, to suppose that changes in the way in which television is paid for or in which programming decisions are controlled could transform television and offset the limitations of the mass society, as long as the payments ultimately must come from the mass society and the programming decisions must be acceptable to the mass society. It is not realistic to believe that the control of television can be isolated from the influences of the public taste and used separately as an instrument for the redemption of the public taste.

But it is realistic to recognize that tastes and standards, like all things in history, have always changed and always will. It is realistic to recognize that tastes vary immensely within the society and that millions of people are prepared to respond to a standard of excellence to which tens of millions do not respond. The great deficiency of television, with its limited number of channels and its preoccupation with the mass audience as a market, has been that it did little for these millions except to offer them occasional meritorious programs at inaccessible hours. But two factors seem to me now to offer a realistic basis for anticipating significant advances in the television of the future. One of these is the technical fact that more channels will be available, and this will alter what I have suggested has been one of the three controlling conditions. Hopefully, it will present viewers with more choice and broadcasters with more competition for the audience. Perhaps it might even destroy the monolithic bulk of the mass audience and lead to a situation where the viewing public, like the reading public, forms a variety of audiences, and chooses from a considerable range of offerings that are really different, rather than between two situation comedies or two crime thrillers that might as well be one.

Perhaps this is only to say that one advance in the television of the future would be actual and not merely nominal competition in programming. As I understand it, it is technically realistic to expect this. Programming which would recognize the range within the audience, rather than treating all viewers as if their tastes and interests were indistinguishable, would be a great advance.

While technical developments are moving to make such a change possible, social developments are, perhaps, also at work to make it more necessary. For there is abundant evidence both that standards of taste are changing and that they are becoming more varied. The measurement of such changes is, of course, intangible; but when we look back to the early films of Mary Pickford, the early radio programs of *Amos and Andy,* the popularity of the novels of Harold Bell Wright, it seems inescapable that the American public has become far less naive, far less limited in outlook, far more aware than it used to be. Some of this awareness may take the conspicuous form of pseudo-sophisticated indulgence in pornography, but a great deal of it is a questing awareness, sensitive to values and responsive to excellence.

Whatever the shortcomings of college students may be today, they are not the anti-intellectual Joe Colleges of a generation ago. Moreover, college enrollments now are so great that the college generation of today will be the American public of tomorrow. Television will be programming for this public, and it will be a very different public from the one which first saw television at the World's Fair in 1939. Looking at the evidence, it does not seem utopian or visionary to suppose that broadcasters who have been inhibited and held back by the audience levels of the past will find release and opportunity in the audiences of the future. Or that broadcasters who have been complacent and unimaginative in accepting the audiences of the past will be stimulated and even jarred and goaded by the audiences of the future.

If these possibilities can be realized in terms of a situation in which selective programming will contribute to upgrade levels of taste, and rising levels of taste will present a challenge to be met by better selective programming, then will television reach the point where it may fulfill its vast potentialities as one of the two great media of communication in the American society.

PAUL GOODMAN

The Social Perspective

I wish to raise some problems and issues about current commercial television. Although I shall suggest some constructive alternatives, I cannot provide them. I wish I could. I am afraid that most of the leadership of the industry, who have the power to provide, will consider the medicine far, far worse than the disease.

The three conditions Professor David Potter describes are extremely important to my argument. There is also a fourth condition which I think is equally important in the history of the development of broadcasting in America, and this will be my main theme. It is that this development took place at a time of increasing concentration of capital and centralization of control and there is a superstition, on the part of the public as well as on the part of the entrepreneur, that the more centralized and bigger the organization, the more efficient the operation and the better the product. With regard to some things like the provision of water supply, I guess this is true. With regard to things like education or communications, it is resoundingly false. Yet the superstition exists, and the accumulations of capital in modern times have served to implement it. With this increase of centralization and control there has occurred, of course, a counter-Jeffersonian, or anti-Jeffersonian reduction of the multitude to passivity; they have no initiative or power to make decisions in most important matters of life, except the choice of commodities on the market. Therefore, they degenerate into something called "masses," with the taste of masses. My theme is not going to be the bad taste of the masses, but the fact that too few minds are in control, and they pander to this bad taste.

Incidentally, one disadvantage of over-centralization of control is that it determines the kind of bad taste; it interferes with the people's natural bad taste. My own feeling is that there are vast numbers of people who would prefer a far sexier fare than NBC, ABC or CBS dare allow for fear of offending some other group. For instance, in the girly magazine business, when *Esquire* magazine reached a circulation of about 600 thousand, the editors had to cut out the more raw stuff. In order to make the leap to a circulation of over a million they had to tone it down and appeal to another crowd. So then another magazine came in—*Playboy*. *Playboy* is a significant magazine because it was the first one that showed a very interesting phenomenon in American life: you can beat the million "sound barrier" with way-out sex. But the television people haven't found this out yet, unfortunately. I likewise think there is a large number of people who would prefer much stupider entertainment than even NBC, ABC, or CBS dare allow. I wish those people would get the stupider entertainment that they really want. You see I am not an elitist. I believe in more variety. I believe people should get what they want in a free market. I hope that our UHF channels will make that possible.

Even more important than the centralization of control is the interlocking of the centralized powers in our society and the lack of countervailing power against the interlock. The broad background is, in fact, that our country at present has degenerated into a kind of feudalism with a strong monarch. General Motors, for instance, employs 600 thousand, a pretty good little barony. NBC, last time I saw the figures, had 220 stations in the network. The New York public school system, to give an example of a public enterprise, has a million children and employs over 60 thousand people, and turns over 900 million dollars a year—a pretty whopping little barony—which is governed by a junta on Livingston Street, New York. For this kind of control over this amount of resources there are just too few minds, even if they were wise and benevolent. It's the nature of our institutions that the wise and the benevolent do not rise to the top; the safe rise to the top for obvious reasons. Consider the newspaper business. In 1900, six hundred towns had competing papers. This year there are, I think, less than fifty. Now the few newspaper chains and a couple of international news services are simply not enough minds to give the news. And so the news the public gets about, for example, Vietnam is practically as bad as that which the CIA gives the President. It's about on the same level of lack of information. In order to find out what's going to happen next month you have to read I. F. Stone or some little independent operator who has no resources whatever, except that he is not caught in the trap of going to the same cocktail party and using the same wire services as everybody else. When I look at the television news at night, it is the same news that I see in the headlines in the morning the next day. I mean exactly the same. Apparently these broadcasters with all their equipment and all their men overseas can't provide anything different. When, occasionally, there is something different—like the burning of the huts at Quang Ngai that CBS caught— it shakes up the country. But this is a one-in-a-million item. To sum up, in our society in general there is an over-centralization of control, and a too tight interlocking of that control, forming a big feudal system with a strong monarch doling out the subsidies. In this situation it is very hard for much reality to exist.

I have nothing against the advertisements or the commercial part of television. On the contrary, my own feeling is that the only part of television which has fulfilled its promise at all is the commercials. It is the only part that has any aesthetic validity. For instance, it's the only part that uses montage the way you would expect a film medium to, which makes the proper use of the relation of music and pictures.

The commercial use of animated cartoons in selling pills, as you know, gives "scientific proof." You see the bubbles rise in the stomach. This kind of handling of the medium should be on television all the time. Also, I should expect any live new art to get real creative artists operating. Apparently all the creative artists are in the advertising agencies who make the commercials. Once when I was television critic on the *New Republic* I suggested quite seriously (though everybody thought I was kidding) that it would be much better if we dropped the programs and stretched the commercials to half an hour. It would be far more authentic. It's authentic because it's about something: namely, someone wants to make a buck. It's for real. In the arts in general, whether high art or low art, unless there is some real motive operating, the result is going to be inauthentic or phony. The trouble with most of the programming is that it is not authentic. The programming does not have as its real aim—and I defy the people in "the industry" to deny this—affecting the audience, either to teach them something or to really move them. The programming attempts to hold the audience in order that the commercials can occur. Now that is not an authentic, intellectual, or artistic motive. And given that motive, the result must be that the packaging is more important than the content. And so it is.

Take providing information or teaching, and consider the Fairness Doctrine. The effect of the Fairness Doctrine is that since equal time must be given to both sides of a controversial issue, it's much better not to have controversial issues. This is, in fact, what has occurred. What's left out of that equation, however, is the realization that the bland is an ideology. When television runs soap operas and so forth that have the sex mores of, let us say, the old *Saturday Evening Post*, television is selling an ideology. I have a right to demand that more rational sex mores get equal time. I tried this with Commissioner Henry and he said, "No soap." It's the same thing with the ads for motor cars. Many of us in community planning think that the present over-proliferation of motor cars is one of the greatest menaces to urban America. Yet television programs continually throw the cars and the oil and the highways and the freeways at people. Unfortunately, we on the other side can't afford the advertising, but we really should have a half an hour a week at least in which to say these things are a menace; they pollute the atmosphere, they congest the streets, they destroy urban patterns, they destroy the countryside. Obviously the accepted, the bland, is not controversial. And promoting the bland or noncontroversial is confirming the worst features of American life. So I don't think the Fairness Doctrine can work, and it doesn't work.

Another objection I have is that networks have tended to regard the channels as if they were *their* property rather than *my* property. My objection is really not that the television industry makes money, but that the networks have taken my beautiful medium, which was developed by my scientific forebears—you know, right back to Gilbert and Clerk Maxwell and Hertz and all those great men—they have taken this medium, which belongs to me, and they have abused it. They haven't used it for the purposes that I would want. For instance, one thing that we hoped for from the time of the Arabian Nights is that we could see at a distance. Television—GREAT! We'll be able to see at a distance. But that's exactly what hasn't been done. The industry is afraid to use the medium out in the world where we can see what's going on, for those programs might be dull, and untoward things might occur; instead, the programs must be under control, and live shows are hardly ever made any more. Shows are taped to keep them more under control. This is a fundamental abuse of the medium. Another thing— which has happened throughout modern society—television technology has outstripped television content. The same thing has happened in modern architecture. Therefore what is given us is mechanical, cold, glossy—it's got no guts. This is a misfortune of modern life.

Television should never have developed that way, it seems to me. Consider the aesthetic failure I mentioned before, when I said the commercials have a better aesthetic surface. In all these years no one has dared to take the screen and give it to somebody like De Kooning and say, "Look, here is how you use the camera. Go ahead. Here's an hour. Make a visual hour." Jean Cocteau would have been a natural for the television medium to give an hour to, to fill it any way he wanted—with surrealism and abstraction. Now, it is not the case that the networks would have lost all their audience on such things. A lot of people would have looked just for curiosity, or to jeer. It would have been what it would have been, but it would have been doing a public service. Doing something for my medium. Getting real artists to try to develop it. As an artist I just cringe when television people talk about their technique—what technique? Any kid can learn it in two years in college. We know that. A real art has a real technique, required in saying something new, the way a great painter has technique, or the way an Eisenstein or Pudovkin has the required talent in cutting a film. I haven't seen that television has made many efforts in that direction except in the commercials.

Consider another kind of subject which is familiar enough, but is very bitterly important to me. Monopoly control in a few hands has led to *de facto* censorship. It really is pretty base when television leaders argue that the government must not come in and censor them, when, in fact, the censorship exercised by television is extraordinary, and they all know it. But every time I complain to the FCC, I get the same answer: No, the networks and stations are totally responsible for what they program and I have no redress. By a recent policy, however, my letter will at least be brought up when they reapply for the channel. But this is just in the past few months. Consider the *de facto* censorship. A few well-known cases will make the point. Many will remember how Albert Ellis's tape, that he and Max Lerner and some

other worthies did with Susskind—I think it was for Metro-media—
was just erased without a word. This was a tape on the sexual revolution that was pretty plain spoken but perfectly clean, nothing obscene;
serious people talking seriously about an important subject and saying
what they thought. I happened not to have been on that panel, but
supposing I had been: what right did they have to waste my time that
way? Who in television can edit what serious people say? They can
ask, is it competent, what they say? An editor has that right. You can
edit for technical reasons, to cut out the dull passages and so forth.
Nobody objects to that. Beyond that there is no right to edit. But that
is not the reason for the editing. Television is afraid of losing this
piece of audience and that piece of audience. That's an abuse of free
thought, free art, and they can't expect an artist to like it. I don't
like it.

Consider another case, where I was an eye witness and could see the
horror of it. In New York, last October 16, we had one of our Vietnam Day Parades (I'm a pacifist). This magnificent parade—we had
nearly 25 thousand people in it—walked down 5th Avenue in New
York. What was the coverage that evening on the three networks? I
went from network to network to see how they covered it. They show
one line of march, eight people abreast. They stick the microphone in
front of one person—"Why are you on this march?" They go over to
the sidewalk where there are hecklers; the hecklers of that march were
about two dozen, about six on every fifth corner, with their signs—Go
Back to Russia or College or Drop Dead—"Why are you heckling?
what is your objection to these people?" As if, in fact, there were as
many hecklers as marchers. This was the coverage. It was a fair balance, perfectly fair. Television gave both sides: one side was a march
representing everybody in the city of New York. These weren't kids,
beatniks, or anything like that—there were 10 per cent of those—but
schoolteachers and lawyers and people from the broadcasting industry,

people from Time-Life. I happened to be walking with some Time-Life people, and with my wife and daughter. The Time-Life people took their pictures and returned to join the parade because everybody except the top brass, in television and in Time-Life, is against the Vietnam War. We know that. Well, balanced with this, were a couple of dozen hecklers. Meantime, there was no overall shot, from a camera up on the roof. What kind of editing is that to send around the country as our parade in New York? The people who put those things together know better than that. That's *de facto* censorship.

Let me harp on Vietnam again. There is a television panel. They are going to discuss the Vietnamese War, so they go as far against the war as who? Hans Morgenthau who is an academic power-politics theorist. The real essence of this war is not power politics, but that half the population of the world is starving to death; that their standard of living is falling relative to ours and falling absolutely; that we come on like a great power to the disadvantage to the rest of the world and to ourselves. Yet the extreme left on the television panel will be somebody like Hans Morgenthau, who accepts all of the premises of power politics. The people who should be on the panel, like A. J. Muste, who year after year has been saying things which have proved to be true, are never there. Now the people in television are not so stupid that they don't know that there is real opinion, but that is not the range of debate they want to show. It doesn't fit the format. That's censorship. I don't mind, if that happens in *Time* magazine. I can print off a paper, too. We can have our own magazine. If we don't sell as many copies as *Time,* that's all right. But television is a semi-monopoly. That's quite a different story. It has a different public duty. And broadcasters are neither willing nor able to perform that public duty, so far as I can see.

The same thing can happen even on WNDT, an educational television station. The day before I came out west here, I was on WNDT on some program about obscenity and I pointed out that one of the most obscene things on the air at present, and far more obscene than any spike-heel novels, is the cutting of the Vietnam story or the Southern story with the ad for a sleek Oldsmobile. This is really obscene. I looked at the program in the evening and the words CBS and Oldsmobile were blipped out. Educational television! I immediately complained. I got back that they cannot make libelous or slanderous statements. Now, in the first place, it was neither slander nor libel—it was the plain truth. It was perfectly responsible criticism. I meant obscene, socially shocking. These weren't individuals I was criticizing. Oldsmobile isn't an individual, it's a public institution, just like a politician or a person who goes into a theater to act. CBS is not a private person. I'm not slandering a private individual. I'm talking about a public institution. And my rights against them are exactly the same as if I say the governor of New York is a crook. I might be wrong or I might be right, but I can surely say so. And if I think CBS and that kind of broadcasting is obscene, I certainly have a right to say so, and it is so. But apparently WNDT has got to play ball. Perhaps not with Oldsmobile, but I suppose with CBS—it's kind of not decent in the industry to criticize that strongly. Will I then be entitled to no criticism of the chief medium?

I followed (I was television criticizing at the time) the visits of Stanton and Sarnoff to Congress to try to get rid of the equal time provision in the national elections. And I just thought, in 1856, if you had had television, Fremont would have had what Sarnoff called quixotic ideas, and there would have been no reason to use a national medium to broadcast the quixotic ideas which four years later elected Abraham Lincoln as President of the United States. Or take the Socialist platform in 1912; the quixotic ideas of the Socialist Party in 1912 were woman's suffrage, the 48-hour week, unemployment compensation, the conservation of natural resources; and in fact, out of fifteen planks in the Socialist platform in 1912, twelve are now law of the land. Yet, if you had had television in 1912 these would have been quixotic—and there is no reason why the quixotic ideas of minority groups should be presented to the American people at the expense of the television industry. Well, I don't want them to be presented at the industry's expense either; get rid of the monopoly and let somebody else do it. Later I'll make some proposals as to how to get rid of the monopoly.

There is also dishonesty within television's own organizations. Let me give two instances. Take the Johnny Faulk case, which we all know. Now during the trial, when Johnny Faulk finally got a 3 million dollar settlement against those who had blacklisted him, high officials of CBS went to that court and confessed that they had been chicken, that they allowed themselves to be blackmailed. Now to be chicken, to allow yourself to be blackmailed is not an actionable offense. It's a moral failing and you cannot send a man to jail for that. I don't think the president of CBS should have gone to jail, but I object strenuously to the president of CBS then going down to the FCC and saying that he is a morally responsible agent to broadcast to the American people.

Even more blatant was the business of the quiz scandal, in which Charlie Van Doren got fired. Now anybody who was a professional could tell a fixed show. And either the president, Mr. Sarnoff, or the chairman, Mr. Sarnoff, knew it was a fixed show or he was irresponsible. In other words, he is a crook or a fool. On either grounds how does he dare to go down to the FCC and ask for a renewal of license? But instead, Charlie Van Doren gets dishonored. Was anybody on top tarred with any black brushes? Was the station censured by the FCC? Was the license suspended for six months? There's dishonesty within their own organization, yet they present an incorruptible image.

I'll give some remedies.

To remedy the last defect, the dishonesty within the organization, there ought to be due process enforced by the workmen within the organization the way it is done in the university. You just can't fire somebody without a trial by a jury of his peers. Every big corporation exercises this tyrannical power from above; and therefore in every big corporation there should be due process. Likewise, there has to be a big change in AFTRA and other unions. They should become real craft and professional unions, to protect the reporter who sends in a news story and feels that it has been unfairly edited. He's a professional and cannot be treated that way as a professional. This is the claim a professor would make in the university. So every professional or craft union in whatever enterprise ought to regard itself not as a union for wages or fringe benefits only, but as a union to help the worker to carry on the profession like a professional. Because they are responsible for what appears, I would certainly apply the same rule at Time-Life, not only on television.

Likewise there could be a check on *de facto* censorship by external pressure groups. I've tried, so far unsuccessfully, to get the AAUP to serve as a watch dog over television. If somebody complains of the violation of fair intellectual treatment, by being wrongly edited or censored, as in the Ellis case, the AAUP will then condemn them and urge all of their professors to stay away from that network. Boycott them. Just the way they do with universities. Also I've tried to form, but unsuccessfully so far, a league of artists. I've tried to get Jimmy Baldwin, Norman Mailer, and Dwight Macdonald, and others, to form a league of artists to say, "They're not going to pick our brains unless they pick our brains honestly." I won't appear unless I appear live, now. I've had it. I've been edited a couple of times too often. In general I'm for decentralization of control in television but there ought to be more centralization where it would be useful, such as in the covering of the Kennedy funeral, the Pope's visit, the election returns, the big sports events, and so on. It's perfectly ridiculous for the stations to be competing on these topics. It's just like the United States and Russia competing in the flight to the moon. It requires just too much capital equipment to compete on that level, and who is advantaged? It's the same whether you watch the rocket go up on NBC or CBS. It is really not worth while to follow the election returns on three networks. The ads like George Gobel at the convention are worth seeing, but then maybe each of the three networks could produce a good ad to cover it.

On the whole there ought to be more actual decentralization. This requires, for instance, giving out the UHF channels, if possible, to independents with the right to co-ordinate freely, the way Pacifica Radio is co-ordinated. But not to form network agreements which do not allow entire autonomy of most of their programming at home. Now I know that this is absolutely unacceptable to the television industry, but nevertheless some Congressmen are fighting for it and I hope they succeed. As many channels as possible, and there are seventeen channels possible in any region, should be given out to real independents and I don't care who in the devil they are, in fact, I would assign them by lot the way the WPA Theater was purely mathematically assigned. I wouldn't care if they were fascists or communists, or any kind of weird group, so long as they were independent. Now, a good many of these groups can't afford to run television stations, although if a station is run independently, it isn't so expensive. Then what I would do, and this not only for the television but also for the mass magazines and the big newspapers, would be to enact a mass medium tax on the size of the audience. The point of the tax is not punitive—it is not to cut down the audience, but just to collect revenue. Start maybe at 200 thousand. If there are 200 thousand listeners or buyers the station or network or magazine pays a tenth of a mil, or whatever the figure would be; and the tax would be graduated, so that when you got up to the 5 million mark the tax would be a pretty good sum. Such a very, very small tax, if collected from Time-Life and CBS and NBC and big movie houses, would come to a pretty piece of change. All of this money would be ear-marked to be used for one purpose only, to underwrite independent media of all kinds: local independent television, local independent radio, little theaters, little magazines, local newspapers. With any kind of rules that make sense, independent ideas would be given a chance to get a hearing. Underwriting a little magazine, for instance, would mean guaranteeing a circulation of 10 thousand for three years. If at the end of the three years the magazine hadn't gotten any place, it would be out of luck. At the end of three years, however, it might have won an audience. The idea is to get rid of the situation where too few minds are operating, and where the control of public information is in too few hands. Incidentally, the mass media tax is not too different from the proposal in the British Parliament to tax the amount of advertising, but that was partly a punitive tax in order to discourage formation of networks or to keep the networks small. I'm thinking of this not in any way as punitive, but just as a means to provide a fund to underwrite independent opinion that will countervail managed opinion. This seems to me to be a very sound constitutional principle. When some institutions, like network television, begin to attack the possibility of American democracy, then it is good if by its very excess, the attack generates a countervailing force which makes possible American democracy again.

Under the conditions I've described, we would find that many more creative and earnest and political people would get into television, and its quality would begin to improve.

DISCUSSION

In sharp contrast to Mr. Ashmore's speech of the day before and Mr. Goodman's speech that was to follow directly, Professor Potter's statements were given with the dispassionate objectivity of the historian. Mr. Potter was not concerning himself in evaluating programs or in judging their possible effects, nor was he trying to fix blame for television's not being better than it is. His purpose was to develop an understanding of television as it is by describing its evolution against the background of events. He showed the forces that have shaped and now control the broadcasting system we have. The audience appreciated this approach. By viewing television through a long perspective each person felt less culpable for whatever unwanted effects television might be having on the American people.

There were few questions and little discussion of Mr. Potter's speech. It was clear, accurate, fair, and hardly debatable.

Mr. Goodman, on the other hand, started his attack at once and the audience was ready to receive it. As we prepare to brace ourselves against an expected blow, this audience was braced. In a sense Goodman's speech began before its scheduled time. He arrived the first day and took a lively part in talk, discussion, and argument from that moment. From the first Goodman and the conferees regarded each other as "the enemy." The battle line was clearly drawn. There was no understanding on either side and there seemed no more chance of bridging differences than there was in Richard Hoggart's description years ago of "them" and "us."

Because of this sharp, immediate, and irreconcilable difference the audience resisted every idea and every argument Goodman put forward. The speech and reactions to it would provide an interesting study in rhetoric. From the point of view of a communicator, however, the situation provided numerous examples of "selective attention," "selective perception," and "selective retention."

Having set out the difficult circumstances of the speech, one cannot then say that Goodman did not have a valid position or that he did not have important criticism to level against television. He did. But, this particular audience was in no way ready to consider his ideas. In a quieter time, removed from the heat of the Seminar, some of the conferees may read the speech and find merit in some of the arguments.

There was no really relevant consideration of Mr. Goodman's speech in the general discussion or in the group discussions later, although there was a good deal of argument *ad hominum.*

TELEVISION IN A NEW LIGHT

MARSHALL McLUHAN

Television in a New Light

Canada is the land of the dew line (distant early warning) system. As the United States becomes a world environment, it has grave need of distant early warning systems as a way of discovering what's happened. Culturally, dew lines are a very valuable device. Two aspects of my operation at our Center for Technology and Culture in Toronto seem to me of special significance to the future of television. One of the things which we discovered in recent months is that in every society, every new environment creates an intense image of the old one; the new one is invisible. *Bonanza* is not our present environment, but the old one; and in darkest suburbia we latch onto this image of the old environment. This is normal. While we live in the television environment, we cannot see it.

I am also mainly concerned with perception—how to see things. Apropos of this, someone said the other day that Canada has no classes, only the Mass and the masses. Canada was created by rail only a hundred years ago, and owes everything to the railway—the joining of French and English Canada together was a railway action. Rail is a profoundly centralizing power. Now with the airplane and television and radio, Canada is coming to an end. A country three thousand miles long cannot be held together by rail while putting up with airplanes, radio, and television, which are decentralizing forces. Separatism is a simple fact of radio and television.

Radio and television, like electric lights, are profoundly decentralizing separatist forces. They give everyone anywhere, whether under the ice of the arctic or here, the same information, the same space, the same facilities. Anyone who talks about centralism in the twentieth century is looking at the old technology—*Bonanza*—not the new technology—electric technology. Our children grow up in a world that is integrated electrically, that is, a world in which everything happens at the same moment. It's an "all-at-once world" of happenings. Then they are put into school rooms and colleges where everything is classified and fragmented—where subjects are not interrelated. And they really are baffled. This is what Paul Goodman calls "growing up absurd." What could be more absurd than to go from an electric, integral world into a disintegrated, fragmented, mechanical world of the old nineteenth-century technology which we call our school system?

In the sixteenth century there was a painter known to us all by the name of Hieronymus Bosch who painted this same dilemma in his "Temptation of Saint Anthony" and other nightmares. The sixteenth-century experience was not unlike ours except that it was the reverse, sort of negative to our positive. The old Medieval world of iconographic sculptural space was confronted by a world suddenly integrated by visual perspective space. So, in the "Temptation of Saint Anthony" you have the old Medieval world of strange icons overlaid by the new perspective Renaissance world of uniform, continuous, and connected space. To the sixteenth-century person, this new world was an outrage because it destroyed every known human value. What we now think of as the basis of our whole civilization—namely uniform, connected, and continuous space, rational space, rational order —was, in the sixteenth century, a barbaric intruder into their order. Visual space was considered the destroyer of all human order. Now we think of it as the basis of all human order.

When electric circuitry comes into play, it creates not a visual space at all, but an all-at-once simultaneous space. Consider the new jokes.

"Alexander Graham Koloski, the first telephone pole."

There is no concept of space, the joke has no starting line, no connection: everything happens at once.

"What's purple and hums?"

"Well, naturally, an electric grape."

"Why does it hum?"

"It doesn't know the words."

These are totally irrational, not-connected stories which our kids love. This is the electric world, where everything happening at once is normal. It is the world we live in and operate in, but not necessarily the world we think in. Our thinking is all done still in the old nineteenth-century world because everyone always lives in the world just behind —the one they can see, like *Bonanza*. *Bonanza* is the world just behind, where people feel safe. Each week 350 million people see *Bonanza* in sixty-two different countries. They don't all see the same show, obviously. In America *Bonanza* means "way-back-when." And to many of the other sixty-two countries it means a-way-forward when we get there.

The electric world of separatism produces a world of disease and discomfort and distress, which has in turn produced a whole batch of jokes. In a wonderful little book, *The Funny Man*, Steve Allen says, "The funny man is a man with a grievance." So, we have the grievance joke—The cat is chasing the little mouse and the mouse finally eludes the cat, dives under the floor and lies there panting while the cat prowls around. After a while everything is quiet. The mouse begins to feel a little more comfy and suddenly it hears a sort of "arf, arf, bow wow" sound and decides the house dog must have arrived and chased the cat away. So up pops the mouse. The cat grabs it, and as she chews it down the cat says, "You know, it pays to be bi-lingual." Another example—The president of Canadian Shell is talking to the president of American Shell a couple of years hence, and the Canadian president is saying, "We must have a big personnel integration program and totally reorganize the whole show." And the American president says, "Say, who do you think you're talking to, white boy?" That is a grievance joke with sort of a double barrel. Humor is a profound area of research and social science because it shifts around with the shifting area of sensitivity and grievance. Slang too is very sensitively responsive to pressures in the environment and thus it doesn't last long: when the pressure shifts, the slang disappears—it fades out. Slang is a spontaneous and natural behavior which records quite deep motivation. Slang, the grievance joke, and the joke without a story line all belong to the electric world, where everything happens at once.

The newspaper is like this. Any newspaper is crammed with events in which there is no story line, no connection between any two events except that which the reader may choose to make. There is a date line —no story line. In an electric world the story line disappears quite quickly like clothes lines, stag lines, party lines, hem lines, neck lines. All forms of lineality disappear.

Television is a very nonlineal, nonstory-line form as a medium. Any story line that television has is borrowed from other media, like the movie which has a natural story line. One of the effects, of course, of the influence of television on the movie is that the Fellini world and many of the new movies do not have a story line. The interchange of influences between television and the movie has been extraordinary.

When television came in it went around the movie form and the movie became an art form. The movie used to be vulgar trash; now it is art. Whenever a new environment comes around an old environment, the old environment becomes an art form: coach lamps, buggy wheels, and model-T's anything. This applies at very high-brow levels. When the machine world of railways and industry was new, it went around the old agricultural world and turned it into poetry. The whole agrarian world became the romantic movement, a great treasure and heritage. Meanwhile the new mechanical world was abominated as monstrous. When electric circuitry came in, it went around the mechanical world and turned the mechanical world into an art form—abstract, nonrepresentative art. Whenever a new environment appears it is spotted as the degrading and monstrous thing and the old environment, which used to be degrading and monstrous, becomes art. When will television become an art form? It is still environmental. A simple answer is, of course, that television is not an art form because there is nothing around it yet. There will be a moment when television will become an art form and everyone will recognize it and realize that it is a great art medium.

The western world organizes itself visually by connective, uniform, and continuous space. The oriental world, antithetically, organizes everything by spaces, by distances between sounds and objects, not by connection. I read the other day a bit of advice to American businessmen confronting Japanese clients: when you sit down with your client, state your business in just a simple phrase and then be silent. Thirty-five or forty-five minutes may go by. Say nothing. Every moment of silence is working for you, because your client is inwardly meditating your problem, your capacity, your pattern. He is deriving huge satisfaction from this inward meditation; if you were to make some connection between your problem and something else, this would destroy the whole show. The oriental works by interval, not by connection, and that is why we think he is inscrutable. We cannot visualize what is happening. And, in the electric world in which we now live, everything occurs by instantaneous little intervals rather than by connections. We are orientalizing ourselves at a furious clip. The western world is going east much faster than the eastern world is going west.

The confusion this creates is reminiscent of the Hieronymus Bosch problem. We all see how the eastern world is acquiring some of our old nineteenth-century technology—tractors and such—but it is not nearly so obvious to us why we should be going east. We cannot perceive our own oriental drift because it is so environmental as to be invisible. We do perceive their western drift, on the other hand, and it does not make us very happy. We figure they must be rivals and so we must deal with them as with any other rivals—crush them. For ourselves, however, we wouldn't know how to prescribe for an illness or distemper such as orientalism in our own midst. It is like *Alice in Wonderland*. Alice was in a world where no visual values existed, where there were no connections and no ground rules she had ever heard of.

This kind of world has recently been looked into by Edward T. Hall in a really fascinating and relevant book called *Hidden Dimension*. Mr. Hall looks at space as it relates us to one another in social life and in entertainment. He has spent a good many years studying the distances which people in different cultures use between themselves in conversation. For example, there is a space used in North America between people that makes it very difficult for husbands to know the color of their wives' eyes. If you ask one of them suddenly, "What is the color of your wife's eyes?" the chances are he won't know. Now, this has something to do with space. Hall has especially noticed that the space used in Arab countries for conversation never exceeds eight inches, the reason being that the Arab must be able to smell the person he is speaking to in order to feel at ease or friendly. If he is unable to smell his interlocutor he at once senses hostility. Hall tells this story. "I was sitting in a hotel lobby in Chicago watching an elevator for a friend to emerge when I suddenly became aware of a strange presence beside me. And this presence kept sort of crowding and being somewhat oppressive and boorish and obnoxious. And I was determined," he said, "not to heed this character and not to be upset until suddenly he was joined by a group of friends and I realized with a sigh of relief they were Arabs." Now, he said, "In an Arab country any sitting person, any stationary person is fair game. You shoot 'em down. Whereas a moving person, as in a motor car or on foot, is sacrosanct, inviolate. You wouldn't dare interfere with a moving object." In America, if you are sitting still, minding your own business, you are inviolate. No one is going to bother you.

Every new medium changes our whole sense of spacial orientation. Since television, our kids have moved *into* the book. They now read five inches away from the book; they try to get inside it. Television has changed their whole spacial orientation to one another and to their world.

If I were to ask the television industry, "What is the business you are really in?" the answer would have to be, "We are in the business of reprogramming the sensory life of North America, changing the entire outlook and experience of the population." This has nothing to do with programs; it has everything to do with the medium. For example, television as a medium is a total antithesis of the movie. In the movie you sit and look at the screen. You are the camera eye. In television you are the screen. You are the vanishing point as in an oriental picture. The pictures goes inside you. In the movie, you go outside into the world. In television you go inside yourself. The television form of experience is profoundly and subliminally introverting, an inward depth, meditative, oriental. The television child is a profoundly orientalized being. And he will not accept goals as objects in the world to pursue. He will accept a role, but he will not accept a goal. He goes inward. No greater revolution has ever occurred to western man or any other society in so short a time. This profound revolution of sensibility and experience came without warning. No one has even noticed that it has happened and the effects of it have created all sorts of discomfort and perturbation and all sorts of questions from the press, but no understanding. The person who sits in front of a television image is covered with all those little dots; all the light charges at him and goes inside him, wraps around him and he becomes "lord of the flies."

Let us contrast this; let us go back for a moment to what happened to us long ago. There was a time in the Greek world when western man was still tribal and still lived almost entirely by ear in the Homeric and Hesiodic world of poetry. There is a wonderful book on this one, too, called *Preface to Plato* by Eric Havelock, in which he describes this transition from the world of the ear to the world of the eye. He got on to this idea of oral versus written culture during his acquaintance with Harold Innis while teaching in Toronto at Victoria College. Havelock is now head of classics at Yale and is the first classicist to have written on this subject as far as I know. The book is really concerned with how people organized their experience before Plato, before writing, and why Plato suddenly took off in the particular way he did in the direction of classified knowledge and ideas instead of operational wisdom of this Homeric type.

The modern connection of this subject is the detribalization, which occurs in any society, and which is now going on in many parts of the world by virtue and benefit of the phonetic alphabet. To detribalize people, push up the visual component in their experience to a new intensity and the ear component dims down. They become detribalized, fragmented people. Owen Barfield has a book on this subject called *Saving the Appearances,* in which he describes the effect of literacy in creating modern civilized man with his values of detachment—objectivity. Before the alphabet, ordinary society was profoundly involved in its experience. Auditory man is always involved, he is never detached. He has no objectivity. The only sense of our many senses that gives us detachment, noninvolvement and objectivity is the visual sense. Touch is profoundly involving; so are movement, taste, and hearing. All of these senses have been given back to us by electric technology. Man is becoming once more deeply involved with everybody.

When Oedipus set out to find "Who done it?" in his tribal society, who performed this heinous thing that caused all the misfortune to Thebes, he began a profound "James Bond" investigation into the criminality of the offense, and he quickly discovered "I done it." One of the peculiarities, you see, of a totally involved society is that everyone is totally responsible. In an electric world you cannot isolate responsibility, for many things may be relevant here. Everyone is so involved in every aspect of everything because it all happens at the same time, at the same moment, by the same technology.

In Truman Capote's book *In Cold Blood,* he describes a world of involvement in which everybody is the murderer of those people, including the author. If there is a real murderer, it is probably the author or the reader, one or the other. No one seems to know. There is no question of pinpointing and saying "He did it, I saw him. Get him. Punish him." Under electric conditions of information it is impossible to say "He done it." It used to be possible to say this under the old conditions of nineteenth-century classification and fragmentation. You could pick out the criminal and punish him, but under electric circuitry where everything happens at once—impractical. It is a little like the change in the dance floor. There used to be a time when people would dance around a space doing fox trots and waltzes. On the new dance floor this doesn't happen. Space has changed. You couldn't ask anybody doing a frug or a watusi for the next dance or for any dance. The dancers make their own space, their own world. They do not share it with anyone and you could not share it with them. This is a new electronic space, which the kids understand instinctively and are miming and dancing. It isn't necessarily bad. It is just so different from anything we have ever known. It is nonwestern. It is noncivilized. It is nonhuman. But it is valid. The electric world has its own ground rules and belongs to our technology—technology which we have made ourselves. All of the technologies that create these new environments are ones which *we* make.

Now this brings us back another step to the difference between the public and the mass. You hear the word mass used a great deal in our world. It is like the difference between the fox-trot floor and the frug-dancing space. The public is a world in which everybody has a little point of view and a little fragment of space all his own, private. In the mass audience everyone is involved in everybody and there is no fragmentation and no point of view. The mass is a factor of speed, not of quantity. This is literally and technically true. The mass is created by speed and everyone reading the same thing or doing the same thing at the same time. It is like Einstein's idea that any kind or particle of matter can acquire infinite mass at the speed of light. Any minute, trite bit of news acquires infinite potential at the speed of electricity. Anything becomes momentous at electric speeds. And a mass audience is an audience in which everyone experiences and participates with everybody and in which nobody has a private identity. So the psychiatrist's couches today are groaning with the weight of people asking, "Who am I? Please tell me who I am." There is no identity left. At electric speeds nobody has a private identity. Don't ask whether this is good or bad. It is an inevitable function of electric speeds. Now I don't think that we have to be all that helpless; we can do something about it, if we are determined.

The public, or *la publique* as Montaigne called it, came into existence in the sixteenth century with typography. It never existed in the Middle Ages and it no longer exists today. Under electric conditions there is no public. There is a mass, meaning everyone involved. How does one conduct oneself in the midst of a mass of totally involved and metaphysically merged entities? Nobody ever asked this question. I personally don't find any satisfaction in complaining about it, or in congratulating ourselves upon it. This is one of those things that really happens: it is a happening. Many people, by comparing or contrasting it with some other condition, in some other part of the world or in some other time in our own world, may or may not take satisfaction in it, but I personally see no basis for that. Montaigne was the first person to discover *la publique,* and he was also the first person to discover self-expression. He said in one of his essays, "I owe the public a complete portrait of myself." As soon as the public exists, the author exists. Until the author exists the public does not exist. They make each other. So, when Montaigne discovered the public, he discovered self-expression at the same moment.

Today self-expression is meaningless because there is no public. There is only the mass. Anyone who attempts to attach artistic importance to self-expression is talking back in the sixteenth or the nineteenth centuries and not about our time. The whole complaint about elite art versus mass art is irrelevant because it ignores the technologies in question. Advertising can be regarded as a profoundly important art form, but it is not private self-expression. The newspaper is a profoundly important form of expression, but it's not self-expression. Take the date line off a newspaper and it becomes an exotic and fascinating surrealist poem. The old idea of elite art, which is now obsolete or useless, was that it was a storehouse of values, of self-expression and self-discovery, of great moments of individual experience stored up as in a blood bank for the use of the community or of the privileged classes. Today the whole idea of art is that it is an instrument of discovery and perception: that real art, valuable art, offers you the means of perception. Flaubert said, "Style, it is a way of seeing." It is not a form of self-expression. Conrad said of his whole life's work, "It is above all that you may see . . . That's why I made it." This is the technique of perception. Art is not a consumer commodity. It is not a package, as it may have been in the nineteenth century. Art is now a way of seeing, of knowing, of experiencing a world, of exploring the universe—like science. The difference between art and science ceased in 1850 with Cezanne. Art, just as much as science, became a technique of investigation and exploration of the universe with Cezanne, Boileau, and Flaubert.

Now, how does one relate art to new media, to television? What is the future of art in relation to such a form? Keep in mind that with typography and the printed word the public came into existence for the first time. Printing was a technique so powerful that it created *la publique*. The manuscript, the handwritten book could not produce a public, a reading public or a market for goods or anything else. With the uniformly produced, repeatable, printed book came, for the first time, a commodity with uniform pricing. Until this time, there was nothing ever produced uniformly with a price on it, except perhaps gold or bronze coins. With the coming of the printed book you get the market and you get the public, and television merges these two entities.

That backward or distant countries have difficulty in forming markets or imitating our way of life need not be baffling. Indonesia or India could not possibly have a pricing system until they have had long centuries of our type of literacy and uniformity. Without our type of uniformity you cannot say "this costs 39 cents." When you say to an Indian or an Arab, "This costs so much, it's a fixed price," he simply considers this a challenge to his dramatic ability. And so if you try to say, "But look, this is the price and has nothing to do with your desire to dramatize your abilities," he will consider himself robbed, deprived, degraded. Our pricing system degrades most countries: it robs and impoverishes their whole way of life. And don't blame them for going into Communism. Communism is the only possible out, just as the PX store is the only possible out for people hurrying into uniform production. Backward countries don't approach Communism as an ideal, they regard it as the only possible means of mechanizing. In this regard, keep in mind that when a new technology goes around an old society the society tends to idealize its old technology—for example when Russia got our western machine world, this drove them back into a furious idealization of their primitivism. So you can depend on it. China will have suddenly emerging within its borders a huge idealistic movement to glorify the ancient China and to downgrade and stamp out all western forms. This is inevitable. We did it to ourselves over and over again, and every country that ever got a new technology always built up an ideal out of the old one. The Romans idealized the Greeks, the Greeks had ideals of spontaneity and barbarism. The Middle Ages idealized the Romans. The Renaissance idealized the Middle Ages—witness Don Quixote—and the eighteenth century idealized the Renaissance. We idealize the nineteenth century. That's our image—*Bonanza.*

Another hypothesis of mine is that *Batman* is a nostalgia for the world of fifteen-year-old experience, a nostalgia produced by color television. Color television is a new environment producing nostalgia for an old one. The old one is comic books. The year of the first comic book in North America was 1935. So we are due for a little nostalgic revival thanks to color television. Color television is also a new technology going around the old black-white. It creates a new experience in our world and will change the whole sensory life of North America. Color television will have many of the effects that color has on other peoples: for instance it will encourage them to cultivate very hot spiced foods. Color television is a world that affects *all* the senses, not *some* of the senses: it is not just a visual form. It will change our sense of hearing as well as our sense of taste and our outlook. It's quite easy, once you know the components of a new technology, to pin-point certain developmental results in a given culture. The effect of color television, for example, in India would be quite different from its effect in North America. It is just the same with radio. Taking radio into Algeria has a very different effect from taking it into England. In England the auditory sense is stepped up to a new intensity in a culture that is highly literate and this has a very different effect from stepping up the auditory sense in a culture that is almost totally auditory, like North Africa. Television has had a very different effect on France from what it has had on us. It has Americanized France; it has Europeanized us. Television has downgraded our visual life and values to the point of *rigor mortis*. It has cooled us off to the point almost of *rigor mortis* politically. On the other hand, television has heated up the French, who are not as visual as we. French television, by the way, has an 819 line picture definition as compared to our 525 line definition. If we used 819 lines, this would help us out of a lot of nasty school problems, right now. Our kids would find school easier because if the visual photographic level of the medium were pushed up a bit, there would be a bridge between their electric world and their school room which would ease their problems. I suggest this hypothetically. But there are many reasons for saying that it is almost certainly true.

Another basic fact about our electric environment: it creates a total environment like the world of the hunter. Man entered the phase of neolithic or specialized sedentary life 10 thousand years or more ago. He sat down and began to specialize and weave baskets, make pots, and grow crops, and domesticate animals. For many, many ages before that he had been a hunter. With electronic technology man becomes a hunter again. Hence James Bond, hence the sleuth, hence crime. Crime in our program world has nothing to do with television as such. It has very much to do with the fact that electronically the whole world becomes a hunting ground for information, data. Modern man is the hunter, and crime and the sleuth are natural modalities of the recovery of his ancient status. The specialist man, the classifier, is not at home in the electronic world. The electronic world rubs out all barriers, all partitions, all classifications. That is why the existentialist discovers the difficulty of having a personality in the modern world. Electrically, you cannot have a private personality. It belongs to an older technology of data classification: for example, "I'm a Hungarian, I'm a dentist, I'm 35, I have three kids, that's me." Under electric conditions that's nobody! People have trouble orienting themselves in this new environment because no one told them that it has new ground rules; the ground rules are always invisible anyway. So, the world of the hunter—our world; the nineteenth century—the world of the planter. In our type of world, the programming of the sensory environment becomes the normal activity of men.

At the Center, over the last three or four years, we have been working on a project called a "Sensory Profile" of the entire Toronto population. We have devised, by the most approved and fragmented and quantitative social science procedures, a means of discovering what are the sensory preferences of the entire Toronto population. Through the speed of learning of our subjects, we have discoverd how long it takes them to recognize a visual, auditory, tactile, kinetic pattern within the same pattern. With all these different sensory ways tied to computer measuring devices, we have been able to profile their whole sensory life and preferences and also the changes in that life over the past thirty years. So we are in a very good position to tell you exactly what happened to the sensory life of the Toronto population when television came in. We would like to do this study in many other parts of the world, because I am pretty sure it is an indispensable resource for decision makers in every field. We would like to do it in Greece before they get television and then afterwards. We would also like to test the effects of other forms on the sensory lives of the people of other countries.

Once you know the sensory profile of a people, how much intensity they allow to their visual life or their auditory life, you can just read it off as a percentage of their whole sensorium. Then you can exactly program the entertainment, or clothing, or colors, or food, or anything for that area. You know exactly what is wanted. While this is neither good nor bad, it might terrify some people. They are going to say, "Who is going to decide?" This reaction is based upon the old technology of fragmentation and specialism.

When this kind of knowledge comes in, people automatically assume new responsibilities. New technologies create new roles and new responsibilities. People respond to these, as our children are doing. Jacques Ellul, in a wonderful book called *Propaganda*, mentions somewhere, on a page or so, that in the whole history of mankind no child ever worked as hard as the twentieth-century child—data processing. The amount of information overload in the environment of the child today is fantastic. No human being ever had to contend with such amounts of information as a daily load for processing. Every one of our children engages in a data-processing load that is overwhelming by any human standards. So what do they do? They find short cuts. Our children become mythic in their whole structuring of reality. Instead of classifying data, they make myths. It is the only possible way of coping with the overload.

IBM were the first people who asked themselves the question, "What is the business we're really in?" They began to look into it and they came up first with negative answers and said, "Well, whatever it is we are not in the business of making business machines. That's not our business." Further study, much further study, and they came up with this answer: "We are in the business of data processing. It doesn't matter by what means, that's our business." So, ever since then they have just gone like a shot because they have not been worried about the particular technology they're using. They know that data processing is permanent and it doesn't matter what technology is used —an abacus will do just as well as nose counting. They added one other thing—"We are in the business of pattern recognition." That's their pet phrase and I think this is the business that we are all in—the business of an electric society is pattern recognition. Now in regard to a normal activity like instruction or education, if you were to ask a teacher, an ordinary person, "What is the business you are in?" he would say instruction; instructing the young. He would be wrong. The business of teaching is to save students' time, not to instruct them. Anyone can learn anything if he has enough time. It's the same with the doctor. A doctor's job or a hospital's job is not to cure people. It's to cure people much faster than they would otherwise get well. It's to save the patients' time. When you know your business, it saves a lot of headaches and a lot of confusion. And I'm pretty sure that when we realize that a new technology completely alters the sensory life of a whole population, we realize that the business of most of us is repro- gramming the sensory life of the population. And when we know this, it creates a new kind of responsibility.

I've often been struck on the west coast by a strange behavioral pat- tern or personal life style which I try to explain to myself by saying, "Well, this is a part of the world that never had a nineteenth cen- tury." There was no big metropolitan industrial time of highly spe- cialized activities with heavy industry and so on. You could say then that the people in the west coast area leap-frogged out of the eight- eenth into the twentieth century, skipping the nineteenth. This is a big advantage. The nineteenth century was the period of maximal frag- mentation and classification. People who leap-frogged out of the eight- eenth into the twentieth century are more imaginative, more flexible,

more perceptive than those who went through the nineteenth. The
nineteenth century was a gristmill that really broke people into little
bits. On the other hand it created many values that do not exist on the
west coast—privacy, separateness, neatness, order of all sorts of visual
kinds. You can see that the environment of parts of California is a
tribute to the eighteenth-century imaginative life. No nineteenth-century mind would tolerate the environment of country left in its natural
state. Nineteenth-century man would tidy up the trees and the tree
trunks. He would level the whole terrain. He would give it the good
old steam-roller treatment. That was the nineteenth century—the
century of the iron horse.

The safety car is an extraordinary indication of the new mood in
America. It's the end of an era. The safety car is a way of saying,
"Look, we're not just interested in the engineering job here. We want
to know, what does it do to people? What's the effect it has on the
people?" And the effect is then built into the car. It is like the safety
pin. A safety pin is made by folding the thing back into itself and
clasping it; that is how the safety car will be made. Instead of just
pointing it out at an environment, you fold it back into itself and
clasp it. The safety car is a revolution. Are we ever going to get any
safety media or safety science?

The future of commercial television raises the theme of the future
of a good many things, including advertising. A student at the Center
wrote a paper for me the other day on the future of advertising, pointing out that it has already got the future written all over it. Advertising is substituting for product, because the consumer today gets his
satisfaction from the ad, not the product. This is only beginning. More
and more the satisfaction and the meaning of all life will come from
the ad and not from the product. In an information environment—the
electric light creates an information environment, so does television—
the service industries take over from hardware and products. The serv-

ice industries are all informational, like advertising. The future of advertising on television is huge because it has to take on the whole job of giving you the product and the effects of the product. Advertising will be participation in the products, understanding and use and satisfaction from them. So the future of commercial television has a whole series of questions tied up in it. Don't try to hold it fixed in front of you, and continue to look at it as if it were going to stay fixed. Television will change totally, just as advertising is going to change, just as work is changing. Work is becoming learning and knowing rather than repetitive job holding.

The book, for example, under xerography, is taking on a totally different character from the printed book. Xerography means applying electric circuitry to an old mechanical process. With xerography the reader becomes a publisher and printer and author. Any schoolteacher can publish her own text for her own class, by taking a page out of this and a chapter out of that and handing it out. The publishers know this and they are panicking. Circuitry means a total revolution in the book—the book becomes a service. Instead of being a package, uniform and repeatable, the book becomes a service to suit the needs of the private person. Each book becomes a work of art, a private production. Even now in Toronto, you can phone the electric information service and say, "I'm working on Egyptian arithmetic and I know a little Arabic and I know a little French; I know a little this and that. Please send me the latest." And they will whisk off a batch of pages and cards to you, Xeroxed and reproduced from all the latest journals in all the countries of the world. It's a service for the schools. So the book, as a package uniformly, repeatably produced is not in electric technology. On the other hand, its being obsolescent doesn't at all mean that it's going to disappear, it just means that the book will no longer set the ground rules.

That's the future of television. With cheap playback and video playback and so on, the future of television will be very much like that of the disc, the LP. Movies will be the same. The future of television also relates to the Laser ray and putting the image in multidimension in the middle of the room instead of on a panel and so on.

The future of commercial television really contains thirty or forty different questions, the commercial one being one of the most illusive because commerce in our world now just means information. Management also is just an information service; it is part of the service industries. Decision making is based entirely on information, and so is medicine. Commerce in our world is taking on more and more of the abstract character of information. The future of commercial television combines the whole lot of marriages of technologies.

Now, I will hazard a guess about the future of the planet. It is not quite as harrowing as you might suppose. When satellites and electric information went around the planet, they created a man-made environment around the planet which ended the planet as a human habitat and turned it into the content of the man-made environment. The same thing will now happen to the planet that's happened to every other environment when it becomes the content of a new environment. It will become an art form. The future of the planet is camp, an old nose cone. You know the story about the two mice in the nose cone. One says to the other, "Hey, how do you like this kind of work?" And the other one says, "Oh, well, I guess it's better than cancer research." The planet as art form is going to get the Williamsburg treatment. All the old nooks and crannies of the planet that used to house strange or interesting phenomena and human behavior will be reconstructed faithfully, archaeologically, and tenderly. The planet will be dealt with as a work of art, you know, where the whole human enterprise began. People will come back from other parts of the world, other parts of the universe to have a look at Plymouth Rock, which should have landed on the Pilgrims, as Stevenson said. And the planet is going to become an old nose cone, an old hunk of camp, an old work of art; and that then is the answer to television. With satellites, television ceases to be environmental and becomes content, becomes art form. As long as it has environmental power it is invisible, and as we notice only those characteristics of it which belong to the old technology, movies. When television becomes an old technology, we will really understand and appreciate its glorious properties.

DISCUSSION

Marshall McLuhan's unusual views of the electronic media and their effects on society evoked considerable interest among the broadcasters. The high level of interest stemmed partly from Mc-Luhan's method of using "probes" and trying spontaneous ideas on the audience. And the reaction of the audience to the probes gave Mc-Luhan a good indication of their validity and, quite possibly, their acceptability.

The audience was particularly impressed by the concept that our present total environment is invisible and produces a nostalgia for past environments—thus the popularity of *Bonanza* and, on a different level, *Batman*. Final judgment was suspended, although many were persuaded in part by compelling arguments and equally compelling examples from film, radio, and television, and from cultural and social changes in current society. The listeners were not sure where total agreement might lead them: what kind of commitment they would be making. Also, there was the suspicion that, although Mc-Luhan's argument was plausible, there may be some hidden fault in the scheme which could nullify the whole theory.

McLuhan assisted this suspended belief by not requiring any particular action from the audience. In his view whether a person favors or opposes his ideas, or whether his ideas are considered helpful or harmful, is completely beside the point. We are in the midst of electric circuitry where everything happens at once and the influences upon society are inexorable. McLuhan's concern was the description of electric circuitry, not its evaluation; and he described with considerable clairvoyance what is taking place in our society at present.

The discussion developed into a further explication of McLuhan's ideas. He held the position that in the electronic age no one is responsible and he used Truman Capote's *In Cold Blood* as an example. This view was very disturbing to some of the audience, since its acceptance means that the development of events in time must be denied and it would no longer be possible to maintain a clear relationship between cause and effect in the fixing of guilt.

McLuhan spoke of the possible future of television in the world of electric circuitry. The television audience would become a work force rather than consumers of programs as is now the case. Problems of any kind could be presented to the audience and possible answers obtained through the use of technology which is even now in experimental stages.

In response to a question McLuhan described LSD as a dislocation from environment, in a sense a medium. He did not, however, advocate its use.

To a question concerning computers, McLuhan maintained that computers are really a method of discovery. The use of computers to catalogue and categorize does not belong in the world of electric circuitry, but rather to the world of clear relationships of cause and effect of the nineteenth century. McLuhan also dismissed the rating systems and the "numbers game" as belonging to nineteenth-century cataloguing, and thus not truly relevant to television.

To another point McLuhan answered that the only audience participation in television and movies is fantasy. Reality in the old art sense of the term is meaningless in the electric world. Reality of the outside as compared to inside fantasy has disappeared, since the concept of outside and inside no longer exists.

A good part of the sheer delight which comes from McLuhan's re-marks is that through his system the troublesome, half observed phenomena of children, western man, social changes, and the media are explained away. Although the McLuhan theory is so different as to be almost bizarre his supporting arguments were drawn from every-day observable events as well as from literature, art, history, and philosophy from the Middle Ages to the present.

While his ideas are difficult to accept, they are equally difficult to reject.

TELEVISION: A PERSONAL VIEW

JOHN R. SILBER

Television: A Personal View

I

Having observed this conference in all its plenary sessions and in several of its discussion groups, I discern a rising mood of hostility to criticism. I note also that much of what I had originally planned to say has been said, and there is no point in my probing your bleeding wounds again. I must also admit to a fondness for being heard when I speak, and I fear that if I harken back to issues raised by Ashmore and Goodman, you will tune me out even if you do not throw me out.

Since I am supposed to offer a personal view of television, I want to tell you something about myself and my qualifications to speak on the subject of television. I have fifteen years' experience. My contact with television began in 1951 when I was a graduate student at Yale University and watched the fights each Friday night at the corner television store. Two years later, coincident with my appointment to the faculty of Yale College, I bought my first television set. In those days a Yale faculty member who owned a television set lived dangerously. In the midst of an academic community, he lived in sin. Nevertheless, in an act of defiance, we put our television set in the living room instead of the basement or the garage where most of the faculty kept theirs, and we weathered the disapprobation of colleagues who did not own or would not admit to owning this fascinating but forbidden instrument.

Now, of course, television has become a respectable and even indispensable article in the academic home. Admittedly, professors of the old school claim that they watch television only for Huntley-Brinkley, political speeches, or an occasional lecture by Leonard Bernstein. And if this isn't true, at least it's progress. So much, then, for my expertise and experience in television.

It is also important for you to know that I speak to you as a philosopher—and that implies certain unmistakable disadvantages. As a philosopher I must acknowledge a very high respect for the rational or reasonable way of thinking or doing things. I feel like a square when I hear Marshall McLuhan heaping scorn on deductive and sequential reasoning, as if it were somehow inferior to the instantaneous meaninglessness of electronic circuitry. I feel so old fashioned in saying that even the speed of light is finite; hence, that there is nothing instantaneous about electronic "thought"—even on the false assumption that electronic machines think. I must remind McLuhan, who knows all this, that human brains lack electronic circuitry or even workmanlike copper wiring, that our poor brains carry neurological impulses by means of brackish salt-water circuitry at speeds well under two hundred miles per hour. And doltishly, but disastrously for the McLuhan thesis, I must point out that human *thought* is no faster in the post- than in the pre-electronic age. Man has been an enemy of time ever since Zeus attacked Chronos, but time has endured and human experience has been ineluctably temporal. The instantaneous is as far removed from human experience as the eternal. I can't forget such facts even in the midst of a hilarious speech by McLuhan, who is surely the funniest stand-up comic in the Western Hemisphere. A philosopher, alas, is bound to earth and to reason.[1]

---

[1] Those readers who have an aversion to philosophy are invited to skip to Part II. Perhaps they will be interested in reading the balance of Part I after they have read Part II.

If we are to converse with any hope of mutual understanding or knowledge, we must agree on a few conditions. First, we must have some humility before logic, accepting the falseness of that which is irrational and logically impossible. If a person's position is shown to rest on or contain contradictory elements that cannot be removed, he is under an obligation to abandon his position. If he refuses to do so, there is nothing more to say to him. If he does not accept rational criteria for thought and inquiry, he cannot be given reasons for doing so. On the other hand, if he accepts reason as a guide, as a necessary condition for sound thinking, he doesn't need them.

If any of you are prone to reject reason or logic as a necessary guide to sound thinking, let me, in desperation, propose this little test. If you think you can do better without your mind than with it, then do all your greatest efforts while you are thoroughly intoxicated, or give yourself a psychic lobotomy like the one we had last night, and see if you then cope more effectively with your most difficult problems. Irrationality never helped anyone come to terms with reality. Radical nonsense, however amusing, is not the way of truth, and laughter alone is no adequate substitute for insight.

We must also be humble, and this is the second condition, before the facts. If I continue to insist that the sun is shining and the ocean is blue, while we all observe that it is raining and the ocean is gray, there is no point in your speaking further with me. There is no point in trying to carry on a discussion with a person who refuses to alter his views when confronted by contravening evidence. One must also be prepared to look at and assimilate new facts, and this may require him to suspend belief on some of his most familiar and cherished theories. If one refuses to look at new facts (like the priests who would not look through Galileo's telescope) he forfeits an essential condition of sound inquiry.

A third condition for rational discourse is shared experience. Unless those engaged in discussion share the experiences necessary to the comprehension of what is being discussed, there is no point in their talking together. I remember the heated arguments I used to have with my best boyhood friend over which was better, a Ford or a Chevrolet. You realize, of course, that we were small boys; neither of us could drive; neither of us knew a camshaft from a piston. But it is sobering to recall that our ignorance did not keep us from arguing or fighting over this issue. And it is frightening to observe how much contemporary political, moral, and economic discourse is pursued in the absence of shared experience on which peaceful, rational solutions depend.

As the fourth condition for rational discourse, we must recognize and try to make correction for the irrational impulses that are influential in all of us. Rationality is not an ever-present defining characteristic of man; rather, it is one of his rarest achievements. If Aristotle had been more empirical, he would have said "Man is the animal who ought to be rational, because he is an animal who, with great effort and good will, can be rational." But the achievement is far too rare to sustain Aristotle in saying that man *is* rational. We must recognize and guard against the wide variety of irrational impulses that make objective, rational inquiry so difficult. In the university, for example, we have learned to discount the bias of parents in their assessment of their children. We must ask farmers to discount their special interests in assessing the merits of parity. And comparable dispassion must be asked of television owners and advertisers when they discuss issues of importance to themselves.

Of the many varieties of irrational impulse against which we must guard, one is of pre-eminent importance. It is the irrationality that is bred of fear. I think it is truly said that fear can, and usually does, produce immediate intellectual blindness. What besides fear could account for the automobile industry's response to Ralph Nader? While flying to Asilomar, I read *Time*—thus showing that I'm no stranger to mass culture—and I noticed the report of Henry Ford's speech about Nader. Ford is reported to have said: "Frankly, I don't think Ralph Nader knows very much about automobiles. He can read statistics and he can write books, . . . but I don't think he knows anything about engineering safety into automobiles." Ford's response to attack is as typical as it is irrational. It may be true that Nader does not know how to engineer safety into automobiles. For that matter, neither does Ford. But Nader's incompetence as an engineer does not disprove his capacity accurately to assess the dangers inherent in existing auto-mobiles and to propose, with the help of expert engineers, safety features that can and should be built into new models. Ford is an intelligent man capable of writing an intelligent speech; he is also a wealthy man, capable of hiring an intelligent speech-writer. So how do we account for the obtuseness of his response to Nader? I think it exemplifies blind defense against attack, the response from fear instead of intelligence.

And so I hope you will not allow yourselves to respond in fear to anything I might say; you must not, since the emotion of fear will prevent you from meeting the fourth of the conditions for rational inquiry. If you and I can meet the four conditions I have proposed, we can anticipate substantial agreement in our discussion. Or if we fail to reach complete agreement, we should certainly be able to arrive at some enlarged understanding of the problems.

Please bear in mind, also, that I am not primarily interested in whether we agree. Agreement is not the pre-eminent value. Ultimately we may hope that rational accord is possible on most serious issues, but discussion, argument, and controversy are essential stages in the development of any sound position. And in a world changing as rapidly as ours, any position that is sound for one day will have to be reviewed and renewed through controversy if its soundness through change is to be assured. We must be prepared to argue with each other in good will, with candor, with all the knowledge we possess, and with due regard for the four conditions of rational inquiry.

For the past two days I have heard you dismiss every objection or criticism of television by saying, "Well, that is just so-and-so's personal opinion." Many of you seem to talk and act as if by showing that a statement is someone's personal opinion, you have robbed it of all objective significance. But it is a mistake to suppose that a personal view is *ipso facto* subjective or that only an impersonal or nonpersonal opinion is objective. All opinions, all theses—whether objective or subjective—are personal. If objectivity is defined by the absence of any trace of the individual human mind, hand, or experience, then objectivity is obviously defined out of existence. The difference between objective and subjective views consists in the extent to which views are supported either by arguments or by evidence such that the views of one person have a claim upon the assent of all other persons. An objective view is one for which such strong support can be given, that other persons ought to accept it, that others have difficulty rejecting it without violating some of the basic conditions of rational inquiry.

Now suppose you have a child who insists that $2+2=5$ no matter how carefully you explain the number system or show him how to count. In a case such as this you do not tell the mathematician that he was wrong in saying that $2+2=4$; you do not tell the mathematician that this mathematical truth is just his opinion or that the child's opinion that $2+2=5$ is just as true as his. Rather you conclude that the child is either stupid or obstreperous. The truths of mathematics are not merely subjective though they are always the opinions of persons. They are not subjective even though there may be differences of opinion about them.

Though disagreement about an issue does not prove that there is no truth concerning it or no basis for an objective opinion about it, there are instances in which disagreement reveals the inadequacy of the support for a position. Disagreement may arise because the problem has not been carefully thought out, because the facts are in dispute, and so on. But even after there is complete agreement on the issues and the facts, disagreement may still continue because the parties to the dispute have personal interests in the issue that are incompatible. One hundred years ago Northerners and Southerners could not agree on a solution to the question of slavery. Agreement might have been impossible even if all Southerners had agreed with Northerners on the moral wickedness of slavery. Lincoln was of the opinion that the disagreement was due largely to the fact that Southerners had a property interest in slaves which the Northerners lacked, and he might have found a peaceful solution to the issue had the Northerners been prepared to assume an equal financial burden with the Southerners in the abolition of slavery. Under such an arrangement, the cost to both sides would have been substantially less than the price paid by each in the Civil War.

With these methodological considerations behind us, let me now propose a philosophical principle of fundamental importance to any discussion of values and, hence, to any discussion of values in television. (My presentation will be so brief that it may sound dogmatic, but I hope I can offer sufficient supporting evidence later in discussion.) We must recognize and accept what I shall call the "dependency principle" or the "nonparasitic principle." This principle is essential to any political or personal philosophy that can claim objective validity. This principle can be variously formulated. We might say, for instance, "One must not fail to provide his share of support for the conditions on which he depends." Or more simply, "One ought not be a parasite." This principle would not be so important were we not continually confronted by individuals who claim special privilege as self-made men. There never was a self-made man because individuals do not develop to self-consciousness, to the level of conscious thought and symbolic communication, without an enormous dependence on other people. Man is not merely physically dependent; he is socially, culturally and economically dependent as well. And therefore if he is to act rationally in accordance with the dependency principle, he must acknowledge his dependence and provide his fair share of support for the institutions and individuals who have supported him. If he is dependent for his existence on a society, he is then obligated to help continue the existence of that society. The man who fails to help provide the conditions of survival for his society while wishing to live himself is in serious contradiction; he refuses to recognize the implications of his dependence. Without society, he cannot exist; hence, if he wills his own existence, he must will the existence of that society on which his own existence depends. This is an old Platonic argument, and I think it is as objective and powerful today as it was when Plato first presented it.

But the principle of dependency is not necessarily or automatically observed. It can be and often is violated. After a man is fully developed and educated he can refuse to support the individuals or the society to which he owes his life and development. That is, he can act irresponsibly with impunity. The implications of this fact for social and personal ethics are profound. This means that ethical or value principles are normative and not descriptive; their validity does not imply their being observed, for men can do what is wrong or bad. Earlier we noted that belief is not necessarily true; now we note that behavior is not necessarily right or good. But the man who violates the dependency principle does not thereby justify his violation. He merely shows that it is possible. And we can still hold him accountable for the violation of the sound principle.

Let me illustrate these points by means of a particularly relevant contemporary situation. There are many medical doctors who, after receiving their education at the expense of the state or national government, assert that all socialized forms of medicine are wrong and refuse to cooperate with Medicare or any other public medical program. But how can a doctor justify such conduct? Can he explain why the society that has spent between thirty and sixty thousand dollars educating him cannot expect him to return a part of this gift in service to other people in that society? The dependency principle does not require that doctors support Medicare or some form of state control of medicine. But the principle does require either that doctors accept leadership from Congress on these issues or that the profession itself devote time and money to the creation of a viable alternative.

This dependency principle provides the basis of most of our civic and familial obligations. As we uncover the network of our dependencies we discover our responsibilities. And of equal if not greater importance, we discover ourselves and separate ourselves off from the world and the society about us by coming to understand the limits of our dependencies. As we become aware of the extent to which we are independent, we become more acutely aware of the problem of utmost concern to every fully developed individual—the problem of the meaning of one's own life.

Every human being wants some sense of his own worth, of the meaning and significance of his life. And because it is so terribly difficult to find a satisfactory or reassuring answer to this question, men try to silence the question by escape techniques. The popularity of alcohol and drugs is largely a function of man's desire to escape from self-knowledge when the failure to find significance in his own life becomes apparent. I do not mean that man uses alcohol primarily or always for escape. He may use it for entertainment, to add pleasure and more meaning to an existence he has already come to terms with. But alcoholism and drug addiction are more commonly modes of distraction for the man who has not come to terms with himself or his basic existence.

The most basic response by men to life is the animal or infantile response of the crassest, most immediate pleasure-seeking. The infant wants immediate gratification of his present desires. And this basic approach to life continues to be dominant long after the person learns to restrain his demand for immediate gratification in order to complete the activities that make it possible. The capacity to delay one's gratification of desires until the optimum conditions for their gratification have been achieved is a mark of maturity. And pleasure-seeking in this more or less adult form has been one of the most popular modes followed by men in their attempt to live meaningful lives. The popularity of hedonism derives from its minimal demands upon the individual.

But the radical inadequacy of this means for achieving meaning in one's life is also quite obvious. It has been refuted in theory and in experience countless times. Hegel's and Kierkegaard's refutations are perhaps as good as, or better than, others. The pleasure-seeker is doomed to failure because he finds meaning only in the momentary immediacy of gratification. The passage of time consumes his moment and all his meaning. He is like a man who tries to make a career of eating ice cream, but cannot find it in eating ice cream, for the ice cream either melts or he swallows it—and either way, it is gone. It must be followed by yet another pleasure. Perhaps a candy bar or another ice cream—and so on to indigestion or boredom. The pattern of this mode of life is repetition. And, as Kierkegaard pointed out, the net result of repetition is boredom, a tired rejection of the value of pleasures after they have been repeated too many times. Don Juan exemplifies this way of life. His insatiable desire to seduce is gratified again and again. But since it is insatiable, it is never really gratified. And its fleeting gratification leaves no residue of order or structure

behind. There is only repetition. This life never provides the fulfill-
ment, direction and meaning in existence that human beings want.
They want pleasure and immediate gratification. But pleasure alone is
not enough. And the boredom and frustration that follow, when
pleasure is all there is, are intolerable.

Aestheticism through the arts is another way of life and another
kind of escape. One thinks of Berenson creating a beautiful villa and
a beautiful life about himself. The pace of repetition is slowed. But it
is a life of possibilities never achieving any necessity. This is one way
of living; but why this way rather than another? And one wonders
whether boredom lurks in the wings. The aesthete often develops a
record collection but then never listens to it.

Intellectualism, Kierkegaard argues, is a third way of life. One can
become preoccupied with intellectual problems as a way of forgetting
that he is a man for whom life poses the problem of meaning. One can
forget the meaninglessness of his own existence by occupying himself
with scientific experiments of dubious import. Countless scientists and
scholars are spending their lives in the search of truths that are irrelevant to them. The intellectual runs the risk of losing all subjective
relevance in a life of meaningless objectivity. What difference does it
make to the working scientist that certain uniformities obtain between
certain phenomena? What is the value of purely objective truth?
Kierkegaard demonstrates the madness of objectivity in his example
of the man who walks down the street with a ball tied by a string
to his waist. As he walks, the ball slaps him on the leg. And every time
the ball slaps him, he says, "The world is round." Of course the man
is locked up. And as he is being put away he asks, "Does the world
require yet another martyr for the round earth theory?" Who cares if
the world is round? Is a man sane if he preoccupies himself with the
search for objective truth, for truth that has no relevance for his own
individual life? The absorption in objective problems can become

nothing more than an escape from self-consciousness and self-reflection, a release from coming to terms with the meaning of one's own existence, another way of living without meaning.

In his search for meaning, man is basically concerned with time. Time is the very matrix of human existence, and this empty or repetitive succession must be given direction and significance. Unlike us, animals are timeless. They graze, fight, procreate and die in an eternal present. But we, because of memory, foresight, and thought, live in a past, in a present, and in a future. We endure. Our basic problem in life becomes that of building a structure or pattern of significance into our lives. The quest for meaning can be stated in terms of ordering the time of our lives in a manner faithful to our temporal natures. This means that since we are in time and growing older, we have different responsibilities, obligations, and proper functions depending on our changing age. A child should be a child and not an adult. An adult should be an adult, occasionally childlike perhaps, but never childish. Our lives are made worse or even destroyed when the temporal order is not respected. A child can be destroyed or his life as an adult made unbearable if he is projected, while still a child, into an adult world for which he is not ready. A child is predominately a presexual creature until adolescence. This biological innocence must be reflected in the organization of society and in the education of the child. In youth the problems of sex are dominant and must receive attention in all our institutions. Special problems likewise attend the aged, and the concerns of an old man have as much relevance to the search for meaning in life as the concerns of the very young.

The process of living, or to be more specific, the process of maturing and of dying, is a process that goes on spiritually and intellectually no less than physically. Just as surely as ontogeny recapitulates phylogeny in the development of the body, the individual recapitulates the race in his intellectual development. That is to say, if the individual develops intellectually and spiritually to a significant degree, he must discover, live with, and then discard basic responses of the race to human existence. In educating college students, for example, I have to expose them first to the claims and attractions of hedonism before this way of life can be replaced by a more profound response to the problem of human existence. I cannot begin by giving them the latest word on the subject of ethics: If I did, they might mouth the right conclusions, but they would be likely to regress to an earlier position. They must live through positions and grow out of them just as they grow notochords and gill slits before discarding them for spines and lungs. Genetic development requires our physical recapitulation of biological history, and the genetic development of knowledge requires our recapitulation of intellectual history. We have substantial choice and control in determining the direction and content of intellectual development. But we are bound to a process of recapitulative development. Unless important stages of thought and experience are learned and lived and rejected, intellectual and spiritual growth is impossible. And there is a rough correlation between the number and quality of the recapitulated stages and the extent and profundity of the individual's intellectual development. Only after living through a developmental process do human beings acquire depth, range, strength, and flexibility as persons.

II

Now let me apply this basic point of view about the centrality of meaning and time in the life of each developing person to the critical evaluation of television. When I give you my assessment of television programs, you may be prone to say "Well, that is just your opinion." It will be my opinion all right, but it need not be *just* my opinion. It may be a carefully considered and well-supported objective judgment. Let us consider a series of examples.

Some programs on commercial television are educational no less than entertaining. They are appropriately judged on the basis of educational no less than entertainment criteria. In education we are concerned to inform the mind and perhaps to develop character; hence, we judge educational shows on the basis of their capacity to achieve these ends. Let us take Hallmark's *Connecticut Yankee* and *Disraeli* as two examples. The *Connecticut Yankee* fails in important respects on the issue of information. Justice Holmes was, above all, a great judge. His opinion in *Gitlow v. New York*, for instance, is of capital importance in the cause of free speech. It is a profound statement of what democracy and free speech really mean. But no one who watched the program heard about *Gitlow v. New York* or saw anything that adequately accounted for Holmes' greatness. Perhaps it is impossible for a mass audience to understand the fine legal reasoning on which Holmes' reputation is based.

But *Connecticut Yankee* has many redeeming features to offset its historical shortcomings. It is good entertainment and technically superb. But, more important, the program handles with insight and subtlety the transition of a man from youth to old age, both his development and his decline. And it portrays the shifts in the balances of emotion and power in a marriage that lasted half a century. One sees quite clearly the different values that waxed and waned in the lives of Justice Holmes and his wife as they passed from youth to old age. The show is faithful to time. In it many of our children see a very old lady up close for the first time. They see how an old man begins to be sentimental and silly. These are essential experiences for American children reared in post-depression, atomic families of never more than two generations.

When I think of our children's ignorance concerning the aged, I wonder how cruel the treatment of the elderly will be in another twenty years. We think the Eskimos are barbarians because they set grandmother out on the ice when she is too old to work, and we pride ourselves on our refinement in sending her to an old ladies' home. What will our next generation do with grandmother? Americans, I believe, are profoundly wrong in thinking that grandparents should not be in the home to help with the education of children and, above all, to show the children what the passage of time involves, and what time will do to them. The *Connecticut Yankee* helps to overcome this loss. At least it shows children the decrepitude of old age. They see old Holmes' falling apart on the screen. It is vivid and intimate. It contributes to our children's realization of what life is like, that death is coming, and that they, too, are in time.

Disraeli was, by contrast, quite excellent in transmitting historical information. The leading figure was obviously much more accessible than Holmes to a mass audience. The people could understand why Disraeli is famous. *Disraeli* was a superbly successful piece of mass education and entertainment, though it had neither the limitations nor the greatness of *Connecticut Yankee.*

In *Bonanza* we have middle-brow to low-brow entertainment and some very fine educational bonuses. *Bonanza* is the fighting rejection of the Dagwood Bumstead image of the American father. It is the perfect antidote to *Father Knows Best* and other idiotic shows that seem designed solely to discredit and destroy the male authority figure. It is fine to have at least one older man who is respected by his sons, and who sets and enforces the limits of their freedom. Ben Cartwright's example of parental responsibility has undoubtedly given moral support to many American fathers. *Bonanza* plays honestly with man's essential character as a creature in time. Time is sequential. A boy doesn't know as much as a grown man, unless the man is defective. The grown man needs to teach the boy, and it is important that the boy accept this fact. Little Joe does. And since the mass audience does not read Emerson's essay on "Self-Reliance," it is beneficial that they can derive its message, after a fashion, by watching *Bonanza*. In one program the plot turns on whether the youngest son will be allowed to fight a duel. The father's reluctance to give the boy his head is very nicely counterbalanced by the older brother's insistence that the kid must at some point be allowed to make his own mistakes. The situation is sufficiently basic to be understood by the lower ranges of the mass audience and sufficiently subtle to satisfy the upper.

But there is one serious danger in *Bonanza*. It is creating another Texas politician, and we don't need any extras. Dan Blocker may be as fine in real life as Hoss is on *Bonanza*. But there is no evidence that his qualifications for public office exceed those of George Murphy or Ronald Reagan. That their talents are modest seems obvious enough, whatever their success at the ballot box.

The Beverly Hillbillies is without appeal to me; yet all of my children seem to like it. And it does reinforce the basic American claim that we are a classless society by showing that money is all that is required for an American to move from one social class to another. And it develops the corollary that there are many ways to get rich (such as striking oil) that require neither brains, hard work, nor the Calvinist virtues. It is clear that a little luck helps. And basically this is sound doctrine, particularly if one remembers that it is a matter of luck (or grace) whether one is talented or intelligent. In this respect *The Beverly Hillbillies* is a wholesome corrective to Goldwater Republicanism and the pseudothought of Ayn Rand. It seems amazing that such straight-forward, simple wholesomeness can be produced in California. The Hillbillies have, moreover, a three generation family dominated by a foxy Grandma who makes a convincing case for matriarchy. She may not be pretty, but she isn't contemptible. And except for the periodic transvestitism of Jethro, whose clothes provide no disguise when he appears as Jethrine, the tastelessness of the "Hillbillies," though omnipresent, never approaches the classic heights reached on the Red Skelton or Ed Sullivan shows.

The Defenders has provided more education and no less entertainment than almost any other program on television, not excluding educational TV. The poison-fruit doctrine, the justification of the Fifth Amendment, the responsibility of the advocate to defend a guilty client, and the issue of capital punishment have been presented with dramatic effect and technical accuracy on this program. When it is viewed without interruptions for advertising, as it is on BBC in England, it has striking dramatic power.

Wagon Train was very good both on religion and race in its early years. I remember in particular a program about an old-fashioned, stem-winding revivalist. To present this man as a faith-healing fraud was a useful service. It may have helped television atone for the presentation of religious quackery at its virulent worst on Sunday mornings.

Gunsmoke has a mixed record. It is too stale to be entertaining, but it continues to have appeal as ritual. Judged socially, it has perpetuated the "Lone Ranger" mistake. In almost every program, it undervalues the importance of social institutions in maintaining law and order and exaggerates the importance of one isolated individual with a good will. It is important to recognize the role of the individual in maintaining law and order, but it is wrong to ignore the framework of legal and social institutions in which that role should be played. *Gunsmoke* is a continual invitation to take the law into one's own hands out of one's concern for civilization. And Matt Dillon is so incredibly incompetent. He is expert only at killing the villain after the villain has killed everyone he wanted to kill. Dillon never shows the slightest comprehension of the value and importance of preventive law enforcement. Kitty tells him that Joe is about to kill Gus. The peg-legged nit-wit tells him, and Doc tells him. Three or four boys on the street tell him. Joe's horse kicks him, and Gus's dog bites him. But to no avail. So Joe kills Gus and then—but only then—Matt rises to his full height of seventeen feet two inches and kills Joe. There is no triumph of law and order; there is only the vindictive pleasure of knowing that the bad guy got his.

But that is not the whole story. Matt Dillon has been superb on the race question. Here, incidentally, is where you missed your chance after Harry Ashmore's speech. Your response to him was like Henry Ford's response to Nader. You tried to say clumsily and unconvincingly that he didn't know anything about television. But you could have made a better showing by saying "Look, Harry, *Gunsmoke* has done more to improve race relations than any group of ministers or public officials in the United States. *Gunsmoke* uses the Indian to establish the rights of the Negro. Every Indian on *Gunsmoke* is a Negro in disguise. People say about Indians what racists say about Negroes. And then Matt Dillon says, 'Now look here; he's a human being'; he makes the Indian his deputy, and the public is educated just a little on the race question." I think Matt Dillon, or the writer, producer, or sponsor of *Gunsmoke,* has made an enormous contribution to the enlightenment of the South and the nation on this question. It is far easier for a racial bigot to accept enlightenment from Matt Dillon than from Martin Luther King.

Now let's talk about some of the really serious faults in commercial television. So far I've been saying very nice things about you. And you haven't complained that I know nothing about television. And you may have noticed that my assessment of various shows has not been based merely on my feelings or subjective emotions, but on basic views of the nature of society and human life. Although I may be mistaken in some of my judgments, my criteria are derived from an analysis of what it takes to develop an individual and maintain a just society.

Turning now to the negative case, I think television has been absolutely irresponsible in its use and display of violence. I do not think you members of the industry know enough about human motivation to play around with violence the way you do.

I am not speaking of shows like *The Man from U.N.C.L.E.* which presents a fanciful, stylized variety of violence. One karate blow follows another, but they are all obviously faked, because it is too dangerous to simulate karate realistically. And *U.N.C.L.E.* has all those terribly bizarre weapons. You never know if Illya is wearing an earring or carrying an atomic bomb, or if when Napoleon picks his nose the room will explode. There is so much whimsey in the use of violence that it becomes a kind of passive, non-violent violence. *The Man from U.N.C.L.E.* is doing good things for international politics, too. The producer's decision to cast only comedians in the spy parts was sheer genius. We all know that *U.N.C.L.E.* is fighting *C.O.M.S.A.T.* or some such sinister enterprise, but the struggle does not evoke national loyalties. No one really knows who are the good or who are the bad guys. The man from *U.N.C.L.E.* always wins, but only for fun, with a light, debonaire touch, and never on behalf of the Grand Old Flag.

The Spillane shows, *The Untouchables*, and the series of Gore Enterprises Unlimited are something else again. In these shows commercial television reveals its utter contempt for the welfare of the community on which it depends. Children, young adolescents, and adults, with blood-lust rising, watch passively as men are killed, cut up, broken by hammers, burned, or beaten into insensibility with fists or pipes or chains. Much of television is just an unending series of violent assaults upon the person. I wonder if we aren't facing the situation that Mark Antony prophesied when, standing over Caesar's dead body, he said,

> Blood and destruction shall be so in use
> And dreadful objects so familiar
> That mothers shall but smile when they behold
> Their infants quartered with the hands of war,
> All pity chok'd with custom of fell deeds;

I am afraid this is already happening—violence has become so commonplace that we no longer find it terrifying; worse, we find pleasure in watching it. Of course, I may be wrong. But I submit that you directors of commercial television do not know that I am wrong. And on an issue of this importance, you would be well advised to know that your unending portrayal of violence is harmless before you inflict it on a community that must avoid violence and respect persons if it is to survive.

Thus far I have focussed on programs, but now I want to speak briefly about advertising. Let me assure you at once that advertising is essential to commercial television, and that both are as American as free enterprise. But we all know that we could have good television programs without having commercial television or advertising; the United States could decide to support a public, noncommercial system through taxation. Or, we could require advertisers to present their ads in blocked, magazine promotions that would not interfere with the entertainment programs. This last system works very well in Germany. All advertisements are in half-hour blocks, and all programs are free from interruptions. But on the basis of the nonparasitic principle, I will admit that the success of German television depends upon its using programs purchased from American commercial television. I will grant, moreover, that the highly competitive American system has advanced the medium far beyond the limits reached by any European country, and that advertising has paid for America's creative experiments. Still, won't you grant that it would be pleasant to view some of our finer programs without commercial interruptions?

These interruptions are trivial aesthetic impedimenta, however, which we can endure. But I doubt that we can survive the transforming effects of advertising upon ourselves and our society. Advertising's only purpose is to create desires, and the commercial success of advertising is proof enough that it can fulfill its purpose. It creates desires that call forth new products; it creates new demands that make old and better products obsolete. National advertising campaigns have produced a nation of insatiable citizens, a nation of good customers but discontented people. Is this a blessing? A person cannot be healthy or happy in a state of insatiability. But how can he be satisfied when he is continually informed of new possibilities, and new ways to spend money? How can he achieve self-restraint when he is continually told that restraint is unnecessary and that easy credit plans are available? Advertising makes our people want what they can't afford, or reminds them of what they have gone too far into debt to buy.

Worst of all, advertising creates the idea that pleasure-seeking and immediate gratification are the best ways of life open to man. These are merely the most infantile and animalistic ways of life. Advertising is so single-minded in its efforts to create desires and encourage instant gratification, that it never bothers to distinguish good from bad desires or good from bad pleasures.

Advertisers prefer to abet the ruin of thousands of lungs rather than forego the profitable cigarette accounts. And look at our automobile advertising. Borrowing the basic concepts of motivation from our leading psychologists and psychoanalysts, we have structured our ads in terms of them. If we are Adlerians, we stress the power of our cars, and the car becomes a totemic source of power for ourselves. If we're

Freudians, the motivation is sex. Whatever our views of human motivation, they are built into our advertising. And behind all the explicit appeals in automobile advertising, we may find an implicit appeal to the death instinct.

But I find nothing in advertising quite so offensive as the corrupt use that some advertisers make of children. A recent and flagrant example is the Cheerios ad in which a little girl of five or six years appears dressed in a bikini. She is put through a series of offensive sexual gyrations. She recites the "virtues" of Cheerios, and then, with a wiggle, says something like "If you'll get your mother to buy Cheerios, maybe you'll get a bikini too."[2] This particular advertisement gave me the same terrible shock I received when I first read Svidrigailov's dream in Dostoyevsky's *Crime and Punishment*. Svidrigailov dreamed of a little girl whom he wanted to seduce, and just as he was about to approach her, she winked at him like a common whore. This was Svidrigailov's nightmare. And advertisers put that nightmare on television! This ad exemplifies what I mean by violating the time of childhood. We have no right to portray children as sex objects. We are not supposed to sell jock straps to little boys or brassières to little girls; rather, we must show respect for the pre-sexual character of their temporal order.

Coffee advertisements are still relatively harmless, but even they seem to be losing touch with reality. Isn't it more sobering than Folger's coffee to think that an American housewife needs Mama Olsen to help her brew a cup of coffee? With even less purchase on reality, Maryland Club goes all out in what it promises the housewife with every cup. She serves a cup of Maryland Club that is said to have "heft." The man who drinks the coffee asks, "Where do you get this

[2] *Editor's note*: The officials of General Mills, having seen the offensiveness of this commercial, had just withdrawn it from the air.

heft business?" and a dirty old man off camera, with a leer in his voice, says, "She'll get it." Pow! The man and woman embrace in a way that foretells an orgy, and I ask: have we contributed to the good life by transforming coffee into an aphrodisiac?

What then are the limits of responsible advertising? Are there any? Do advertisers in their pursuit of wealth have the right to misuse our children, encourage use of harmful products, create insatiability, encourage over-spending, and corrupt our sense of the true nature of things? Do advertisers have the right to divert the nation from its proper goals and distract it from its basic needs?

It is profoundly important that our country find a solution to the problem of poverty. If families with incomes under $3000 a year had the homemaking skills and the self-restraint of the average European family, they would have some chance of getting by. With $3000 a year a family could enjoy nourishing food, but it would have to eat oatmeal rather than Cheerios. Advertising, unfortunately, has made oatmeal obsolete, and is making our people want to spend more money for less nourishing food. How can we help our ignorant poor while television advertising teaches them to prefer the expensive worse over the inexpensive better?

Perhaps we may take solace in the scriptural assurance that our poor shall always be with us. But I am far less confident that our democratic form of government will survive unless commercial television is transformed. Without radical change, we shall see the development of a plutocracy in which the people have no effective voice in the selection of political candidates. We will continue to have elections between two candidates. But the only candidates will be those who can find the financial support to pay for a television campaign. Candidates who cannot find such support will have no chance of being elected.

Consider what this means in a state like Texas. It costs $25,000 to be on statewide television for thirty short minutes. Ten appearances cost one quarter of a million dollars. If one advertises his television appearances in newspapers to gather the maximum audience for them, the cost climbs to $400,000. In simple English this means that no man without private wealth can hope to compete for statewide office in Texas unless he is prepared to sell his office to someone or some group.

So the aspiring politician goes to see the contractors to talk about what he will give them and what he will get in return. Then he goes to the labor unions to find out what kind of deal can be made with them. And he discovers that he can be bought by both sides. If his major support is from liberal groups, he may expect contributions from conservative groups that want to take out insurance in case he wins. And vice versa. He also discovers that the same firms that have supported him are also supporting his opponent. And before long he discovers that both he and his opponent are talking very much alike on every issue because they have made essentially the same deals with the same people to finance their campaigns. The high costs of television campaigns are forcing all candidates toward the dull middle of the road, because major financial support comes from essentially middle-of-the-road groups.

Unless we free our candidates from dependence on the monied interests, we shall forge, in spite of ourselves, a system very like Russia's. Instead of a central committee of a party, a central committee of business and financial interests will select all candidates by deciding which men will receive campaign funds adequate to allow them to appear on television. Two men very much alike will be selected so that the financial interests will get their man no matter who wins, and the people will be left with a vote but without a choice.

Now you have my evaluations and grave doubts about commercial television. From the point of view of the individual, television is both a cornucopia and a Pandora's box. I am convinced that an opportunity is matched to every problem. But what are the steps that will eliminate the problems while actualizing the opportunities?[3]

III

The solution to the political crisis that I have just described demands passage of legislation to require the provision of free time by major networks and individual stations for political speeches. Congress must redefine the relationship of stations to the networks and make stations more responsible to them. If the networks are required by law to broadcast a certain number of speeches by each major candidate for national office, there must be some way to require stations affiliated with the networks to carry the speeches.

In local races the equal-time provision can be made to work if each candidate for a given office is required to post a bond sufficient to cover the cost of all broadcasts should he fail to receive a certain percentage of the vote. The requirement of a bond would either compensate the station for time used by cranks or discourage cranks from using broadcast time.

As a compromise measure, stations and networks might be required to provide a certain number of hours of time for candidates in congressional, senatorial, and gubernatorial races in which there are no more than two or perhaps three candidates. Congress needs to begin at once to experiment with a variety of solutions to this critical problem. And commercial television will be well-advised to cooperate in this. Otherwise, the government will be forced to establish a government network, along the French pattern, to solve this problem. It is quite

[3] *Editor's note*: At the conference Professor Silber concluded his talk before he proposed his solutions, saying that he would not bother the audience with his views unless they asked to hear them. After a coffee break he was asked to propose his solutions for a variety of problems. In this printed version he has replaced the question-answer form of the conference discussion by an expository version of his proposals on a few central problems.

clear that voluntary action by networks and stations is unsatisfactory. They have consistently failed to meet their obligations, as Mr. Henry has shown with careful documentation in the *Congressional Record*.

It is far more difficult to find a way for the networks to increase variety in programming. I have been appalled by your reports of the intensity of competition between networks. We cannot introduce experimentation and radical novelty into network programming unless we can reduce the competition between networks. If you would stop competing with such intensity for over-priced talent, production costs in television would certainly decline. There is obvious duplication and waste under the present system. It may be necessary to introduce specific alterations in the antitrust laws to encourage greater cooperation and reduced competition between networks; national interest might be far better served if, as a result, more variety and daring were introduced into programming. And special labor laws will probably have to be written to permit use of student talent by networks.

Perhaps the best way to provide greater variety in programming would be to decentralize an important part of our television system. I think we must establish a national education network that is independent from both governmental and commercial control. It should be financed by means of a special licensing tax on every television station. This tax should be graduated according to the income of each station and should produce at least 100 million dollars per annum, or a million dollars annually for each of the one hundred affiliated stations. Commercial networks and stations would be prohibited by law from making any direct money payments to stations in the educational network.

In order to encourage the greatest amount of local civic pride and in order to encourage individuality and variety in our mass culture, each station in the educational network would be required to produce one-third of its programs from talent recruited within the range of its antenna. And these stations would not be barred from using professional talent, such as union musicians, in productions directed and staffed by students.

The best programs produced by local stations would be broadcast nationally by all stations in the educational network, thereby filling out their schedule of programs while encouraging smaller communities to develop theaters and orchestras in order to participate more fully in the cultural life of the nation. These programs might effect a great national awakening as we become aware of our resources of talent, scattered throughout one hundred different areas instead of concentrated in New York and Hollywood. And we might then be able to view television offering the novelty and variety that has been driven out of commercial television by uniform, competitive programming. The new network might even encourage the rejuvenation of commercial television by bringing abundant new talent to the attention of commercial producers. Under most adverse circumstances, an independent educational network could not fail to increase decentralization, variety, and interest in television production in America. Under most auspicious circumstances, it might provide the stimulus for an entirely new national awareness. It would not replace, but it would substantially supplement, and perhaps transform, commercial television.

DISCUSSION

By the time John Silber made his appearance the conferees had been pretty well battered through attack and counterattack. Silber chose to disarm his listeners by setting forward a broad philosophical base on which he was to structure his comments about television. His comments on specific programs were of real value to the audience. Here was an able philosopher analyzing programs on the basis of their contribution to or their subtraction from the value system of society. Program producers and buyers alike were hearing television discussed with a useful, new approach.

In direct contrast to McLuhan's concept of "all at once" electronic-circuitry happenings without regard to time or space, Silber posited sequential, linear events which must develop in the fullness of time. A hard, but inescapable choice was presented to the conferees. Silber's views based on philosophy and Christian ethics rang with positive authority.

The only question remaining, and it is a basic one, is how well the Silber or the McLuhan approach describes the second half of the twentieth century and prepares us to live in it and to manage it. Is the age of reason with its categories and its causal relationships still valid, or are we, as McLuhan says, now in an era so different from everything we have known before that we must find a new set of terms to describe what is happening to us?

 THE FINDINGS

The members of the Seminar were divided into discussion groups of eight to ten members. Each discussion group was led by a faculty member and a *rapporteur* was appointed from the group. Each *rapporteur* recorded the central ideas which emerged in his group and reported them on the final day to all the conferees in plenary session. The work of the *rapporteurs* is summarized under appropriate headings. These findings were not conclusions for more often than not there was no consensus.

A Commission on Communication

The Ashmore proposal for a commission on communication was received with little enthusiasm. It was generally felt that a commission would probably not be able to interpret popular tastes and the needs of the audience accurately and in a manner appropriate for effective use by the broadcaster. In one group a form of government commission was discussed. While there was some division on the Ashmore suggestion there was unanimous opposition to a government commission of any kind. Almost by a process of elimination the thinking turned to the idea of a group within the industry; this would ward off any outside commission and perhaps forestall future government investigation. The internal study group could report the methods of program selection, what is being done to improve programming and to improve the medium of television. Upon receiving the report the industry as a whole could decide proper courses of action.

Television Programming

The general feeling was that, although they may be subject to some criticism by some parts of the general audience, television programs in total are much better than they were ten years ago. Even so it is essential that the television industry recognize the fact that program standards are being questioned and that they could be higher. A way must be found within the commercial structure to encourage everyone —producers, networks, advertisers, and critics—to work for higher standards. If all elements of the television industry and the allied fields work together the programs could be greatly improved in the future.

Diversified Programming

In the future there will be more diversified programming through the development of community antenna television systems, the increase in the number of UHF stations, and the use of satellites. While there is value in this development from the standpoint of the viewer, it raises several significant issues. The more programming is diversified the more the audience is fragmented. Advertising would be forced into selling specialized products to specialized audiences. A far more staggering problem is that of programming and qualified personnel. Networks, stations, and program producers, who are now hard pressed to provide legitimate fare to fill thousands of hours, would have to meet a new demand many times greater than at present. The truth is that we lack creative material and creative talent.

Talent

It is well understood that television uses up talent of all kinds at an enormous rate and new sources must be found. It was felt that the universities should take the lead in encouraging more people to go into television as writers, directors, performers, editors, and cameramen. It must be recognized, however, that students are sometimes reluctant to enter television because it is difficult to make an individual contribution early in a career either as a writer, or director, or producer. Writing is one of the key needs. There is no shortage of material; there is a shortage of good material. There is no shortage of writers; there is a shortage of qualified writers. Yet the universities cannot do the job without help. A beginning is being made through a few scholarships offered by the industry, but these are not nearly enough. The industry must find the means of providing financial help, internships, and basic equipment to assist the universities in educating people for television. It is a matter of regret that the most powerful medium of information is not very effective in promoting recruitment into its own ranks.

The Cluttered Air

The conferees discussed at length the ever-repeated charge of over-commercialism. The consensus was that neither the time nor the number of commercials has in fact increased in network programming. However, the nonprogram material—such as "credits," announcements of programs to come, and additional mention of other products sold by the same sponsor—has increased. On the face of it, almost all of the "hitch hikers," "cow catchers," "billboards," and "credits" could be dropped away. This would give the viewer a less cluttered air and the sponsor a better setting for his commercial announcements. The questions are which items are to be dropped and how is this to be accomplished? No one favored the idea of scheduling the commercials in special blocks and presenting the programs without interruptions.

A second consideration is that of presenting programs not designed for television. A theatrical film, for example, in its opening scenes is often slow by television standards, and frequently the first commercial break is held off for thirty or thirty-five minutes. The result is that more commercials are placed in the latter part of the film. The frequent interruptions during the rising action cause the audience to become irritated. Different standards might be set up for the inclusion of commercials in entertainment not specifically designed for television. For example, several commercials might be put together at wider intervals during the entertainment portion of these programs.

Programs of Quality

Almost everyone was of the opinion that programs of high quality should be provided. The question turned on how to accomplish this goal and this was left unresolved. The periodic efforts to provide high quality fare have met with little encouragement from the general public. The public simply does not watch these programs in sufficient numbers to justify their production. It may be, as some argued, that the cultured few have avenues other than television to satisfy their needs. However, this truism evades the issue, because television is becoming "the complete medium" and it must attempt to satisfy all needs of the public including the need for quality programs.

Escalating Costs

The critical point about costs is not that they are rising, but that they are rising faster than the growth of the audience. Since television exists in nearly every home and the sets are in use nearly six hours a day, there seems to be little hope that the audience can be measurably increased. This would indicate that if the costs of programs continue to rise, the cost-per-thousand viewers would become so great as to force advertisers from television. The responsibility is hard to fix, for costs are increasing at all levels and in all elements: talent, technicians, writers, producers, networks, and stations.

No single element in the industry can do much to hold costs under control, except perhaps two. The sponsor, finding that the costs are too great, can refuse to sponsor expensive programming. The networks can turn away from programming which has become too costly. However, since the rising costs are the responsibility of everyone, all levels of industry should work toward reducing them.

Network Coverage of Special Events

One of the apparent competitive wastes in television is the almost exact coverage of special events by each of the three major networks. While some pooling of effort has taken place in the past, it was argued in the group discussion that even more could be done. Although some events are of such overriding importance that the public should be given no viewing option, most elections, conventions, space shots, and the like may be covered collectively or by a pre-arranged rotation system. The revenue saved could support other special coverage, news, or public affairs.

Communication among the Communicators

There is a general lack of adequate communication existing on three levels in commercial television: among the constituent parts of the industry, between the television industry and the universities, and between the industry and the general public.

There was unanimity of feeling that the Seminar itself was an excellent way of establishing a dialogue among the various interrelated parts of the commercial television industry. Even apart from the formal presentations made at the Seminar, there was great value in sponsors, advertising agencies, program producers, and television people meeting and exchanging views. In some cases the conferees were meeting their counterparts in other aspects of the business for the first time and learning how each contributes to the grand design of commercial television.

The idea was expressed more than once that there was a general lack of understanding between the television industry and the academics concerning the functions of television, its complexities, and the difficulties faced in trying to reach its goals. One remedy would be to invite industry people to the universities to describe their work; another would be to invite the members of the universities to appear on television, where they might come to know the dimensions of the medium.

Finally the television industry must find more and better ways of developing understanding and appreciation among the members of the general public. In short, it needs better public relations in the broadest and best sense of that term.

✳ CONCLUSIONS

During the Seminar a number of important ideas were expressed. The views were, more often than not, divergent, and it is difficult to take an accurate bearing or steer a straight course through them. The disastrous tack is to weather each gust as it blows, as has often been done in the past. Voltaire in *Candide* recorded a series of events, each more calamitous than the one which preceded. Rising out of each disaster, the character Dr. Pangloss still insisted that this was "the best of all possible worlds." The temptation is strong to rise up from each critical barrage and to maintain that "this is the best of all possible television worlds." Of course it is not. Some kind of clear and balanced view must be achieved.

Television is sheer magic. What person can help but marvel each time he turns on the switch and the little white dot appears in the center of the darkened screen, expands, and then gradually becomes a picture? An event happening at some distant place suddenly appears in his own living room. The critics have said again and again that television has not lived up to its bright promise. Indeed it hasn't. Even so it has taken advantage of the "magic" in many ways, as every honest person can testify.

The trouble is that television with its many facets is difficult to think and talk about. How does one approach and control it? It is as though one man alone were trying to raise the main tent in a circus. The moment one part is raised another part slides down. The sponsor is bound to view television from the point of view of his product and how well it is sold; the advertising agency looks at television as a medium among media and he must represent the best interests of his client; the networks and stations are concerned with the program, the audience, the time, and the competition; the independent producer is involved with the show, the talent, and the placing of the program before the public. Each necessarily looks at television in terms of his own special interest. The critic, too, scans television from his own mountain top and is concerned with intellectual, educational, cultural, and social influences. Each critic may be right according to his own point of view, but television cuts across the spectrum and it is most difficult to assess the total medium.

The question becomes one of obtaining an overview in which we see the whole, the total picture. Yet television is not static: once one sees and understands it, it has changed. Television is a kaleidoscope and the bits and pieces of advertising, sponsorship, sales, shows, culture, news, products, and programming shift, drop away, and reappear in different combinations. A changing, mobile model is needed to illustrate the changes that are continuously taking place.

One method of approaching an overview is through programming, for regardless of the operant forces, the program that the public sees is the final product. Programs might be considered as drama, film, literature, art, music, talk, or dance; each of these has its own structure and is manageable within its own sphere. The trouble is that television draws upon every category and out of the potpourri makes a show. The established guidelines for assessing any of these areas get hopelessly tangled when the same approaches are used for television. It is this kind of situation which lends credence to Marshall McLuhan's dictum. "The medium is the message." Television gives a special stamp to any structure it uses.

Television has been described as the most powerful means of mass communication. But this generalization is not helpful since it could be argued that television is not communication nor is it mass. The delayed "feed back" discourages any sense of interchange between the sender of the message and the receiver. The mass audience may number millions, but each person receives the signal as an individual. The unit size of the audience is just one, two, or three persons and they do not react as would an audience collected for a play, opera, movie, or speech. Specious as this kind of argument may be, it does serve to show again that television does not fit neatly and squarely into the accustomed patterns of thought.

The audience for television seems to be tangible and here we have some quantitative measure. Thus program ratings have assumed a great importance within the industry. By these means we can determine with a degree of accuracy how many people are watching a given show. Unhappily, even if the numbers are reasonably accurate they can supply us with only one factor in decisions to be reached about any given program. If we are willing to pay we can get more meaningful data about the audience. It is possible to learn the age, sex, religion, education, color, and income. What we do not know is what this audience is doing or thinking or how it is reacting to the program.

The deceptive thing about current quantitative measures is the fact that the audience shifts and changes. The numbers of people watching a program over a period of time may shift radically or may remain relatively constant. That is not the point. Nor does the point have to do with the other usual modes of description, for the audience does not change markedly in age, sex, religion, education, income, and other such factors. The point is that, no matter how large the audience, it is made up of individuals and the individuals change continuously. Every person is not a single individual, but rather several individuals. No person is a simple combination of parts; rather he is of a most complicated composition. The composition may vary in accordance with how a person views himself at a given time or may vary in accordance with the people he is with and his reaction to them. It may vary with some interest in which he has involved himself. For example, a man might be a conferee at a Seminar, a business man of power within his own organization, a loving family man, a tough competitor in sports, and an avid connoisseur of the arts. Housed within the mind and body of a single man might be an interest in literature, music, art, dance, drama, theater, politics, and both spectator and participation sports. Within this same person may be the complete moral spectrum from good to evil. The psychologists have told us that if you step on a person's foot often enough and long enough he becomes a potential murderer.

This view of man as a complicated and many faceted individual bears upon television in several ways. How we assess the audience and how we program are examples. Several years ago John Morris, Director of the *Third Program* of the British Broadcasting Corporation, pointed out that the audience for this most highly intellectual radio program in Britain was divided into almost equal thirds among the upper class, middle class, and lower class Englishmen. Throughout the whole class structure of British society there were those who listened regularly to the *Third Program*. In some way each man, whatever rank or class or part of society, must have in him an aspiration for cultural attainment.

The concept of an audience made up of individuals who within themselves range widely in interest and capability, and who are ever changing does not make television programming any easier. Yet, assessing audiences in this way would make it possible to upgrade the level of all programming and to carry the audience along. Because of the complex nature of man he is capable of accepting a number of possibilities we have never allowed ourselves to consider because we have been mesmerized with numbers and transfixed with the idea that the audience is slotted and locked into definite categories. Indeed, if we could shake ourselves out of our fixation on numbers, the other more valid factors of individual and audience composition would properly become the important determinants in program building.

We know too that everything we see and everything we do is a part of our learning process and that we learn whether we wish to learn or not. Everything that happens to any individual has an educative force and those who are engaged in any aspect of television know this. The most pragmatic businessman learns this truth through advertising and sales. Television does influence; television does educate. Commercial television is the great extracurricular classroom of the nation. If we are all teachers, we are obliged to take the complicated man and leave him in better circumstances than we found him; we ought to try to suppress the evil and to develop the good in him. Although those associated with commercial television may be teachers without certification, they are at the same time businessmen working for a profit.

How then do we improve programming? The great fear, and it is not entirely irrational, is that if one follows the advice of the intellectual critic and offers only high-level programs the mass audience may be lost. If television loses the mass audience it loses the power for cultural good, educative good, or sales good. Is the suggestion then to fall right back to the practice of the numbers game? No. The suggestion is that the complex animal, man, is capable of a vast variety of improvement. We can make a gradual improvement on every possible level with the help and even the insistence of the sponsors, advertising agencies, networks, stations, and independent producers. This is not to say that all programs ought to be the same or that all programs must be of high quality. It is to say that within every genre of program now offered or which will be offered a gradual and continual effort should be made for improvement. If the leadership of each of the parts that make up the television industry were to accept this concept, improvement would follow. The conduct and performance of the crew of a naval vessel is a reflection of the captain of that ship. If the "old man" decides upon a new course of action, the "word" spreads through the ship in a matter of minutes. If the leadership in television were to decide for a gradual, continual effort toward improvement the "word" would spread rapidly throughout the industry. The change would be welcomed everywhere for no one really wishes to dedicate his life to a level of production or performance of which he is really ashamed.

But agreement in principle does not in itself bring action. Throughout history, at every turn of the road, there has been one man with one idea that has made the great change in events. That has always been the beginning. If one man would exert his leadership to translate valid principle into action, others would follow. Cooperative effort must be galvanized by the one man who is willing to take the action.

We must accept television as a communication instrument, intricate in design, operation, and use. There are no short cuts in arriving at an understanding of its commercial or social ramifications. Both those using television for profit and those seeking its cultural attainments look for simple formulae. Only if men of stature dedicated to television and the public it serves work patiently together can the tangled skein of conflicting purposes and opposing views be reconciled. Then television will come nearer to fulfilling its great promise. That is what this Seminar was about.

 CONTRIBUTORS

HARRY S. ASHMORE is chairman of the Executive Committee of the Center for the Study of Democratic Institutions and chairman of the Executive Committee of the Fund for the Republic. He has been editor in chief of the *Encyclopaedia Britannica* and is currently a *Britannica* editorial consultant. He graduated from Clemson College, was a Nieman Fellow at Harvard University, and holds honorary degrees from Oberlin and Grinnell. Mr. Ashmore is a distinguished journalist who has worked on newspapers in Greenville, South Carolina; Charlotte, North Carolina; and in Little Rock, Arkansas. He received the Pulitzer Prize as editor of the *Arkansas Gazette*. He has also received the Sidney Hillman Award and the Freedom House Award for his work. His books include *The Negro and the Schools; An Epitaph for Dixie;* and *The Other Side of Jordan.*

STANLEY T. DONNER is professor of communication and chairman of the Department of Radio, Television and Film at The University of Texas. He is a graduate of the University of Michigan and took his M.A. and Ph.D. degrees at Northwestern University. He taught at the School of Speech, Northwestern University, and was associate head of the Department of Communication at Stanford University before coming to The University of Texas. He has had wide experience in radio and in television and was the producer of two award-winning television series. Professor Donner received a Fulbright Research Grant to Paris in 1955–1956. He was also a Fulbright Lecturer to the University of London, 1963–1964. In 1956 he was the

U.S. representative at an International Meeting on the Cultural Exchange of Radio Programs at UNESCO in Paris. He has written for scholarly publications here, in France, and in England. He was a contributing author to *Educational Television: The Next Ten Years*, and to *ETV Problems, Performance and Promise*. He was editor of *The Future of Commercial Television 1965–1975*.

PAUL GOODMAN is a social and literary critic, playwright, poet, and artist. He was at one time television critic for the *New Republic*. He teaches at the Institute for Policy Studies in New York and Washington. In 1956 he was the student-chosen visiting professor at San Francisco State College. In 1964 he was the Distinguished Scholar (in Urban Affairs) at the University of Wisconsin. He is a graduate of City College in New York City and took his Ph.D. at the University of Chicago. Among his books are *Growing Up Absurd*; *The Facts of Life*; *Compulsory Mis-education*; *The Community of Scholars*; and *People or Personnel*.

MARSHALL MCLUHAN is professor of English at the University of Toronto and director of the Center for Culture and Technology. He is a graduate of the University of Manitoba where he also took his M.A. Degree. He then went to England where he took an A.B., M.A. and Ph.D. at Cambridge University. He is best known for his unusual ideas about communication and how the mass media affect people. Professor McLuhan has been given a 100-thousand-dollar appointment at Fordham University for the academic year 1967–1968. Articles about Professor McLuhan have appeared in such publications as *Harpers*; *Life*; *Maclean's Magazine*; and *Ramparts*. His books include *The Mechanical Bride, Explorations* (with Edward Carpenter); *The Gutenberg Galaxy*; and *Understanding Media*.

LEONARD S. MATTHEWS is executive vice president of Leo Burnett Company, Inc., of Chicago. A Kentuckian by birth, he took his B.B.A. degree at Northwestern University where he graduated *summa cum laude*. Mr. Matthews was with the A. C. Nielsen Company for two years before he joined the Leo Burnett Company. There he has moved from one position to another to his present position of responsibility.

THOMAS MOORE is president of television, American Broadcasting Company. He was born in Mississippi and attended Mississippi State College, the University of Missouri, and the University of Southern California. He was given an honorary degree of Doctor of Laws by the University of Alabama in 1965. His rise in television has been a steady progress of increasing responsibility. From sales manager of CBS Television Film he moved to the American Broadcasting Company first as vice president of programming and talent and later as vice president of the television network. He has been president of American Broadcasting Company Television since 1963.

DAVID M. POTTER is the Coe Professor of American History at Stanford University. Professor Potter is a Georgian by birth and graduated from Emory University where he was a member of Phi Beta Kappa. He took his M.A. and Ph.D. at Yale University and later received an M.A. degree from Oxford. He has received honorary degrees from Emory University and from the University of Wyoming. Dr. Potter has taught at the University of Mississippi and Rice University, and served as professor of American history and fellow at Queen's College, Oxford. He taught at Yale University until 1961 when he moved to Stanford. Among his books are *Government and the American Economy*, which he wrote with T. G. Manning, and *People of Plenty: Economy of Abundance and the American Character*.

AUGUST PRIEMER is head of media, marketing research, and advertising administration for the S. C. Johnson Company. He graduated from Duke University as a Phi Beta Kappa. After graduation he spent a year at the Sorbonne and then received a Fulbright scholarship to the University of Aix-en-Provence where he studied the influence of nineteenth-century impressionists on twentieth-century poetry in the English language. After a short period with *Encyclopaedia Britannica* he worked with Proctor and Gamble Company in Cincinnati. He became a media consultant and later joined the S. C. Johnson Company as media director.

GEORGE SCHAEFER is president of Compass Productions, the company responsible for a number of stage, film, and television productions including the *Hallmark Hall of Fame*. Mr. Schaefer was born at Wallingford, Connecticut. He took his bachelor's degree at Lafayette College where he graduated *magna cum laude*. He attended Yale Drama School and has since been associated with television and Broadway productions. Among them were "The G.I. Hamlet," "The Linden Tree," "The Heiress," a revival of "Idiot's Delight," "Southwest Corner," "The Apple-cart," "The Body Beautiful," and "Teahouse of the August Moon." In television he is best known for the *Hallmark Hall of Fame*. Mr. Schaefer has received many awards, such as Show of the Year in 1960 and 1961; Best Director, 1959 and 1961; and Director of the Year, *Radio TV Daily*, 1957 and 1960.

JOHN R. SILBER is professor of philosophy and chairman of the Philosophy Department at The University of Texas. He graduated with honors from Trinity University and took his M.A. and Ph.D. degrees at Yale University. He taught at Yale before coming to The University of Texas in 1955. Professor Silber received the Students' Association Award for Teaching in 1957, a Lemuel Scarbrough Foundation Award for Excellence in Teaching in 1958, the Morris Ernst Teaching Excellence Award in Arts and Science in 1964, and the E. Harris Harbison Award for Distinguished Teaching by the Danforth Foundation in 1966. He was given a Fulbright Research Grant to Germany in 1959–1960, and an American Council of Learned Societies grant-in-aid in 1963; and he was the recipient of a John Simon Guggenheim Memorial Foundation Research Grant to England in 1963–1964. His special interest is Kantian philosophy and he has written *Kant's Ethics, The Unity of Form and Content;* he was editor of *Religion within the Limits of Reason Alone,* and contributing author to *The Ethical Significance of Kant's Religion.*